Aimee Byrd equips readers in the lost art of discernment. You don't need to agree with Aimee on all of the fine points in order to learn from her. Aimee provides practical tips for reading, learning, listening, and discerning.

—**Rosaria Butterfield**, author, *Openness Unhindered and The Secret Thoughts of an Unlikely Convert*

Aimee Byrd calls for men and women in the church to take the discipleship of women seriously. Some pastors have a bad habit of failing to engage women in the church or scrutinize what they study, and male church leaders often fail to be open to contributions from women in the church. This book offers several practical ways for pastors to overcome the separating out of women's ministries, which has resulted in a sort of pink and flowery ghetto of theology.

—**John McKinley**, Associate Professor of Biblical and Theological Studies, Biola University, La Mirada, California

Aimee Byrd fearlessly takes on a range of problems that are not often addressed in the same work: women's ministries and women themselves who lack proper theological training; pastors who neglect the training and the gifts of the women who could be deployed in the kingdom to great effect; and the hyper-complementarianism that is itself bad theology. May all those who need to hear her message give it heed.

—**Kathy Keller**, author, *Jesus, Justice, and Gender Roles: A Case for Gender Roles in Ministry*

Aimee Byrd writes with wit and wisdom, biblical clarity and theological maturity. What she writes about here is a matter of urgent pastoral concern to every minister and elder. There are movements and ideas around that are offering solace and encouragement to those who would hold back our sisters in Christ from being all that they could be for him. Women are our most committed resource for doing the work of the kingdom, and they deserve our best thinking and support. It is our solemn duty to guard all the flock of God, to nurture and use their spiritual gifts, and Aimee helps us to identify and address the issues head on.

—**Liam Goligher**, Senior Minister, Tenth Presbyterian Church, Philadelphia

Unfortunately, many of the answers offered to women today about their place in the church are the result of asking the wrong questions. Fortunately, Aimee Byrd is asking the right questions—tough questions, to be sure, but questions that are much needed and long overdue. *No Little Women* steers the discussion about women and the church back to its rightful place by uniting a high view of Scripture and a high view of women.

—**Karen Swallow Prior**, professor of English, Liberty University, Lynchburg, Virginia

NO LITTLE WOMEN

NO LITTLE WOMEN

Equipping **All Women**
in the Household of God

AIMEE BYRD

P&R
PUBLISHING
P.O. BOX 817 • PHILLIPSBURG • NEW JERSEY 08865-0817

Portions of this book have been taken from the author's writings on her blog, www.housewifetheologian.com, and revised and adapted for this format.

Printed in the United States of America

Library of Congress Cataloging-in-Publication Data
Names: Byrd, Aimee, 1975- author.
Title: No little women : equipping all women in the household of God / Aimee Byrd.
Description: Phillipsburg : P&R Publishing, 2016.
Identifiers: LCCN 2016032784| ISBN 9781629952567 (pbk.) | ISBN 9781629952574 (epub) | ISBN 9781629952581 (mobi)
Subjects: LCSH: Church work with women. | Christian women--Religious life. | Women in Christianity.
Classification: LCC BV4445 .B97 2016 | DDC 253.082--dc23
LC record available at https://lccn.loc.gov/2016032784

I dedicate this book to the core women
in my first Bible study:

Brooke, Caty, Dana, Andrea, Evie, Corie, Jackie, Lora,
Erin, Monique, Courtney, Paula, Lori, Beth, Jill, and our
beloved Kathie, who is now with Jesus.

It was a great honor to study God's Word with you.
And it has changed my life.

CONTENTS

ACKNOWLEDGMENTS

I want to thank all the competent women who have inspired me and have reflected Christ in so many ways. There are way too many to name from among my family, my church, the churches I visit, my friends, and those I have met through my blog. I thought about so many of you while writing this book. I *tested* some of the content for *No Little Women* on my blog, and I want to especially thank those of you, both men and women, who contributed in the comments. Thanks also to the many great women authors and bloggers. I am thankful for your work. You sharpen and inspire me.

A special thank you goes out to those who have helped with the manuscript. Thanks to my pastor, Francis VanDelden, for meeting with me as I was organizing my ideas for the book and for offering good advice and encouragement. I appreciate your taking a critical look at the first three chapters of the manuscript. Thank you to my elder Dave Myers for reading my manuscript with such interest and feedback. I am so grateful for the conversations that we've had, the time you've invested, and the care you've put into this important topic. Also, thanks to Liam Goligher for picking up the phone and calling when I asked for some literary advice. Thank you to Dr. David Silvernail for inviting me as a guest speaker to discuss preaching to women with your communications and preaching class at Reformed Theological Seminary, DC. The material for that talk morphed well into the last chapter of *No Little Women*. I could write a whole chapter on how men like these model what I am writing about and how the church has benefited from it.

Thank you to my editor, Amanda Martin. I love the way that you push me and question me to grow as a writer and communicator. It's all the more exciting working on a book when I have such a great editor to sharpen me. And it makes the process of writing less lonely. And somehow my project manager, Aaron Gottier, always makes editing less painful. Thanks, Aaron, for making sure there isn't any Big Trouble in *No Little Women*.

Thanks to Carl Trueman and Todd Pruitt for giving a housewife theologian a seat at the table to talk about theological issues, not only on the Mortification of Spin podcast but in everyday life as well. You make great spiritual brothers—older brothers—balding, bitter, older brothers. May God give you eighties rock band hair in the new heavens and new earth.

And most of all, thanks to my husband, Matt. You treat me like a competent woman even when I'm falling apart. I strive more eagerly and take more risks in life because you treat me as though you see much more in me than there really is (except when I'm driving, of course). Thank you for the encouragement and much-needed support that was indispensable for me to get through this project.

INTRODUCTION

We read books for different reasons. But whether we pick a fictional, historical, biographical, doctrinal, or self-help book, we are after a positive experience. There is something noble about reading—even if it isn't quality reading—in an age that is captivated by visual media. Picking up a book comes with an intended purpose, one that requires more discipline than reading a blog article, perusing our social media news feeds, or even committing to watch a movie. Reading takes more work. And we want to be rewarded for it in some sense. What expectations do you have for this book? What do you hope to learn? That's a question we will return to later.

When we are talking about Christian books, we really expect results—positive results, even eternal results. And yet, as noble as the art of reading is, it is not neutral ground, not even in Christian publishing. This is a book that aims to help the whole church by examining church initiatives for a group that makes up over half of our congregations—the women.

It's good news, really. I'm not writing as someone offended or burned. I am an advocate for the local church. I am writing as one small person who represents this group of more than half the church. I am a woman. I am happy to be a woman who is a member of a faithful, confessional church. I'm not exactly young anymore; I've grown as a woman in this environment. And yet I'm not one of the women we look up to who are the most experienced in life and have so much wisdom to offer. I'm somewhere in between, having just celebrated my fortieth birthday, creeping up closer to my twentieth wedding anniversary, and having three children who are still in the home, albeit two of whom are going through the confusing teenage years. This seems to be a good time for reflection in life. I can look back at my own naïveté, bad circumstances, mistakes, sin, and occasional glimpses of providential obedience and good timing in the Christian life, and I am also at a good place to look ahead, hoping to wisely apply what I've learned, God willing, to my own family and to any who may care to learn from a semi-crazy, yet informed and venturing, sister in Christ. It's also an interesting time in history for women and the church. While we believe we are in a more enlightened age than our ancestors, we are still trying to decipher and work our way through basic issues such as gender distinctiveness, sexuality, women's roles in the church and home, family dynamics, discipleship, and the relationship between church and culture. I want to encourage readers that there is good news about all of these related and important issues in life. But as you already know, because you were obviously concerned enough to read at least this introduction, there is some critique that needs to be evaluated, even in the places where we would like to take refuge, such as Christian publications, parachurch organizations, Christian radio, blogs, and even the ministries we try to build in our own churches.

Some of this is uncomfortable to talk about, but we aren't called to be comfortable. So I'm not writing in some kind of alarmist tone. I am writing because I know that God has ordained that we often grow in a slow process. My own life is certainly representative of this fact. Some people seem to be blessed with a faster track to maturity. I have often learned the hard way. But I value that learning and don't want to make it any harder than it has to be, especially for those who are younger than me. I want them to learn much quicker! Even so, younger people have a voice that we need to listen to as well. Whatever our age and experience, we are valuable to the church of Christ, and he wants each one of us to be competent in our knowledge of him and in our understanding of the gospel. I still have a long road ahead, Lord willing.

Jesus Christ loves his church. That is the great news I want to share with you in this book. We believe that, right? In fact, Christ loves his church so much that he wants all of his church, including the women, to "attain to the unity of the faith and of the knowledge of the Son of God" (Eph. 4:13). And, of course, we believe that too. But how does Jesus do this for all of us? That is where we begin to have some differences.

Our theological views about creation, gender, and the household context affect the way we think about women's status, roles, and contributions to the church, home, and society. There has been a lot written on these topics, ranging from good to horrible. Many books written for women in the church, whether good or bad, are never read by the elders, pastors, or laymen. Women's ministries have become a sort of separate entity in the church, and this is one of our biggest problems.

As someone who speaks at women's retreats in different churches, I have been blessed to meet many wonderful women who have great intentions to live faithful Christian lives. Talking with many competent women in the faith is always an encouragement, especially when I am able to witness their conversation and life examples. Yet I have also talked with many women in the church who lack important skills in discernment for discipleship. I've also talked and corresponded with numerous pastors who would like to serve the women in their congregations better and to encourage them in using their gifts. But often there isn't clear communication between women's ministries and church officers. All these conversations have led me to ask some questions that I aim to answer in this book. It is written both for women and for church officers, as well as for laymen who care about these matters:

- How does God describe woman?
- Should the church have women's ministries?
- Are women's ministries the best way to serve the women in the church and for the women to serve in the church?
- Is every member of the church a minister?
- How does the church minister to every member?
- Are the women in the church being properly equipped in the Word?
- What happens when women teach bad theology?
- What are the responsibilities of the head of a household?
- Can men learn from women?
- Have we lost the skills to read for understanding?
- Is there a difference between preaching to (and pastoring) men and preaching to (and pastoring) women?
- What is our responsibility in sitting under the Word?

This book is for the competent women who are seeking a better way, as well as for those of you who would like to become more competent, as God has called you to be. This book is also for pastors and elders who would like every member of their church to be well equipped in the unity of the faith and the knowledge of the Son of God. I hope that all men in general will be interested in this significant matter of women and the church. I write with my eyes on the new heavens and the new earth, where we will worship God together in resurrected bodies, forever praising our King. Our blessed Father has set his love on all his people, sent his Son into a fractured and broken world infested with sin, and bestowed on all those who believe in him new life in his Spirit. We are united in Christ. To God be the glory!

The best pastors and elders I know are learners. While they have so much to teach us, God can use even a housewife theologian like me to get a conversation going on this important topic. You will see that the chapters in the first three parts of the book have subsections directly addressing church officers in relation to the material of that chapter. This doesn't mean that pastors shouldn't read the sections directly addressing women or that women shouldn't read the sections addressed to church officers. I take this direct approach because we need to be listening to one another. Pastors, you need to hear what I am saying to the women, and women need to hear what I am saying to pastors. The whole book is meant for both men and women, laypeople and church officers, to read.

The fourth part of the book is very practical for all readers, ending in a chapter addressing pastors on the topic of preaching to and pastoring women, with a subsection for women about sitting under the preached Word. My hope is that this book will help both pastors and elders to shepherd the women in their congregations, and to encourage women to thrive under the ministry of Word and sacrament, so that it flows out to the whole church, to their homes, and to their communities.

PART ONE

Pinpointing a Real Problem

THE DANGER IN
WOMEN'S MINISTRIES

Every now and then I get a disturbing email from a pastor or concerned woman about the women's ministry in their church. The usual scenario involves a group of well-intentioned women studying a popular book that is marketed for women's ministry groups, and it is full of bad doctrine. But the author is extremely likable, she has done many good deeds in the name of the Lord, and, frankly, the women in the group are now invested. They are offended that someone is questioning what they think has been an edifying study. So you can see how this email usually comes after significant damage has already been done.

Or has it? Why quibble over words when these women are bonding by studying a book that many other good churches are using? Because the truth of God's Word is important, and the women in God's church are important. What we study together in a side room of our church or in our living rooms shapes our own growth in holiness as well as the growth of those around us. Women are very influential both in God's

household and in their own. And there are many books marketed to Christian women that appear to be godly, while a
closer look reveals that they are not in accord with Scripture.
But the problem goes deeper than bad "Christian" books marketed to women.

There seems to be a pattern that has gone on from the
beginning of time. We read in Genesis 3:1, "Now the serpent
was more crafty than any other beast of the field that the Lord
God had made." And what is the very next line after we have
been given this information? "He said to the woman, 'Did God
actually say . . . ?'"

In his malevolent shrewdness, Satan went for the woman.
He went after Adam's gift from God, his bride. That was
indeed a clever way to get to Adam. So it isn't surprising today
that Satan goes after Christ's bride, his church, with the same
distortion of God's word.

Are there any sections of Scripture that make you uncomfortable to read and especially to discuss with others? There's
one particular passage that gets to me, and it should be troubling to any pastor or elder in God's church, to any husband
who wants to love and care for his family, and to every
woman who professes the name of Christ. That passage is
2 Timothy 3:6–7:

> For among them are those who creep into households and
> capture weak women, burdened with sins and led astray by
> various passions, always learning and never able to arrive at
> a knowledge of the truth.

This is a jarring warning. It comes in the context of Paul
warning Timothy about false teachers infecting the church.
They have an appearance of godliness, he says, but discernment shows that they are rebelling against the true power of

godliness in the Spirit (vv. 1–5). The assertion that they target weak women may seem insulting at first glance. Of course, Paul is not making a blanket statement about all women. Let's look into the word usage, cultural context, and exposition of this passage in more depth.

False teachers are a serious threat to God's church. In the Sermon on the Mount, Jesus warns, "Beware of false prophets, who come to you in sheep's clothing but inwardly are ravenous wolves" (Matt. 7:15). This is exactly what Paul is describing in detail to Timothy when he warns him about the difficult times we are in during this age of "the last days":

> For people will be lovers of self, lovers of money, proud, arrogant, abusive, disobedient to their parents, ungrateful, unholy, heartless, unappeasable, slanderous, without self-control, brutal, not loving good, treacherous, reckless, swollen with conceit, lovers of pleasure rather than lovers of God, having the appearance of godliness, but denying its power. Avoid such people. (2 Tim. 3:2–5)

And these are people in the church! They are deceptive. And they need to be avoided. Notice how these false teachers—we could even call them messengers of Satan—"creep" into households all stealth-like and target specific women. The language should make us think of a certain serpent.

We read Genesis from our point of view and cannot believe that Eve was so easily deceived. However, we are all susceptible if we are not adequately conditioned in the Word and if we do not look to God to supply us with all that is good. Think about this text for a minute. Paul is exhorting Timothy, the pastor of the church in Ephesus. This is a church known for its passion for the truth! If Timothy needs to watch out for deception and false teaching in his congregation, then so do pastors today. No matter how good the preaching is that we sit under, we are all vulnerable to false teaching.

One way that churches invest in their women and provide a setting for them to serve others is through a women's ministry program. You would think that every church would want to have a strong women's ministry. After all, women usually make up more than half of the church. And we want our women to be active members of the church body. But with all the opportunities for churches to have a thriving women's ministry, this verse in 2 Timothy is extremely pertinent. In many cases, women's ministry becomes a back door for bad doctrine to seep into the church. Why are there still so many gullible women? Have we made any progress in equipping our women to distinguish truth from error in what they are reading? Do the women in your church actually have the skills to lead a Bible study? Why is it that so many women sit under good preaching and have all the best intentions, yet fall prey to the latest book marketed to them that is full of poor theology? And why do so many women in the church fail to see that theology has any practical impact on their everyday lives?

There are several ways to look at this, but let's start by looking at the idea of "women's ministry" in the first place. Through the church's good intentions to minister to every member, we have swung the pendulum too far over into "every-member ministry." In doing this, we have lost our focus on the actual ministry itself. This book isn't a call for churches to ditch their women's ministry programs. Rather, I am asking both the officers and the women in the church to evaluate their women's ministries according to Scripture and also to encourage biblical women's initiatives in the church. I would love for this book to help build up the entire church, both brothers and sisters in God's household.

How do I respond to those emails that make me so sad? I sure wish that women (and men) in leadership would have enough discernment to recognize bad theology. Many don't. And we can all be sharpened. This is an opportunity for an elder to step in and teach these skills. Instead of just saying, "This book is dangerous because of A, B, and C, so therefore you must stop reading it," step in and read it with them. Find out what is so appealing about the book, and get to know the women studying it. Come prepared for discussion, with good questions and Scripture, so that these women will walk away with some tools for discernment. Teach them how to look for what this author is saying about God, about man, and about God's Word. People need to learn how to read a book.

Why We Are So Insulted

Perhaps when you read the words "weak women," your shoulders go back, your eyebrows furrow, and your lips purse. Paul's audacity here provokes a reaction. Such strong language does make some women defensive. This is indeed a jarring warning to read about a particular type of woman. Who would want to be one of those women? I don't want that for anyone in my church. I wouldn't want to hear that about any of God's people.

This expression, "weak women" (or "gullible women"), insults us. It is meant to jar a particular type of woman. The phrase, literally translated "little women" or "small women," was a term of contempt. Paul isn't soft-pedaling the issue here. And he isn't being chauvinistic. His writing in Scripture shows a high view of women and much appreciation for their service to God. I wish we could all be the kind of woman who is praised in his writing.

And Paul is not saying that men are never gullible. He is

saying that a particular type of immature woman was being targeted by false teachers looking to manipulate and infect households. Why do you think they were targets? Let's look at two reasons for going after women in general, and then two that make these particular "little women" even more of a target.

The Value of Women

The very first false teacher, Satan, deliberately went after the woman in the garden of Eden. Why didn't he approach Adam? Was it because Eve was more susceptible to error? Scripture doesn't tell us the reasoning behind his strategy, but we are told that he was "more crafty than any other beast of the field" (Gen. 3:1). Adam was the federal representative for mankind. His obedience would have earned blessing for us all, and his disobedience brought depravity and death to his whole posterity. So, make no mistake, Satan was going after Adam. He was going after Adam by going after his bride. He went for a target of value to bring about Adam's fall.

Before God created Eve, he declared that it was "not good that the man should be alone; I will make him a helper fit for him" (Gen. 2:18). There has been plenty of discussion about this word *helper* in regard to a woman's role, and even to her value. But we don't really attach the same meaning today to this word, so maybe we lose some of its significance. The word *helper* can often bring up connotations of inferiority in our culture. Think of mommy's little helper in the kitchen. Isn't it cute that she wants to help mommy? Let's give her a bowl with some ingredients to stir and have her fetch a few things from the fridge. But don't let her near the stove or the sharp knives! She's just the helper; she might hurt herself!

Of course, this is not what "helper" means in Genesis 2:18. In fact, the same word is used to describe God as a "helper" to Israel throughout the Old Testament.[1] And when we look at these verses, we see that this word communicates great strength. Psalm 89:17 is particularly interesting: "For you are the glory of their strength; by your favor our horn is exalted." Here we have our word *ezer*, usually translated "helper," translated instead as "strength." These verses are also saturated in military language as they describe God as Israel's *ezer*. The root for this word is used 128 times in Scripture, meaning "rescue" and "save." It refers to God's rescue in thirty cases, which we see mostly in the Psalms.[2]

Women derive value first and foremost from being made in the image of God (Gen. 1:27). But, as fellow image-bearers, we have a particular value in our relationship to men as well. John McKinley prefers to interpret *ezer* as "necessary ally," asserting that God has given us this analogy between himself as *ezer* and woman as *ezer* to focus on their functional correspondence.[3] This is certainly different from the way we use the word *helper* today:

> The issue in *ezer* is neither equality nor subordination, but distinction and relatedness. She is to be for the man as an ally to benefit him in the work they were given to do. Just as *ezer* tells of God's relatedness to Israel as the necessary support for survival and military perils, the woman is the ally to the man, without which he cannot succeed or survive. Unlike helper, that could seem optional, and allow the man to think he's otherwise adequate for his task without the women, the distinction of ally marks the man's dependence

---

1. See Ex. 18:4; Deut. 33:7, 26, 29; Pss. 20:2; 33:20; 70:5; 89:17; 115:9–11; 121:1–2; 124:8; 146:5; Hos. 13:9.

2. See John McKinley, "Necessary Allies: God as *Ezer*, Woman as *Ezer*," lecture, Hilton Atlanta, November 17, 2015, mp3 download, 38:35, http://www.wordmp3 .com/details.aspx?id=20759.

3. Ibid.

upon her contribution. This dependence is plain when we consider Israel's need for God's contribution as her ally. . . . What sort of ally is the woman to the man? She is a necessary ally, the sort without which he cannot fulfill humanity's mission. Certainly the woman as a necessary ally fits for the mission of family building. The pairing of the two terms *ezer* and *kenegdo* brings a meaning that is larger than gender complementarity and union for building a family. Necessary ally brings into view the joint mission for which the male and female are created to rule God's earthly kingdom.[4]

Ezer is the word first used to describe a woman's function. This helps us to understand why the crafty Serpent spoke to Eve. Immediately following a description of the Serpent as "more crafty than any other beast of the field that the LORD God had made," we learn that "he said to the woman . . ." (Gen. 3:1). To get to Adam, Satan went after a target of value to him. It is no surprise, then, that he is still relentless in trying to deceive Christ's bride, the church, through false teachers, ill-placed priorities, felt needs, fear tactics, and coping mechanisms, to divert them from resting in Christ and in God's wisdom, provision, and sovereignty.

The Influence Women Have in a Household

Women are influential, both in their personal households and in the household of God. Research shows that men open up and have deeper conversation when a woman is involved.[5]

---

4. Ibid.
5. "Ladd Wheeler, professor of psychology at the University of Rochester, found that women and men are both less lonely when they spend time with women. The data showed that whenever a woman was involved in an interaction, both individuals disclosed more about themselves, and the interaction became distinctly more intimate" (Dee Brestin, *The Friendships of Women* [Wheaton, IL: Victor Books, 1988], 16).

God has given us a gift of being relational. But this can also be used in a sinful way. Our propensity for intimate conversation helps us to be persuasive. This is especially true with our husbands. Before the movie *My Big Fat Greek Wedding* popularized it, Spurgeon gave this witty advice to a bride in a wedding ceremony he was officiating: "According to the teaching of the apostle, 'The husband is the head of the wife.' Don't you try to be the head; but you be the neck, then you can turn the head whichever way you like."[6] It's funny because it's kind of true. We don't have to be the head to have power. But let's not have weak necks!

The saying "Happy wife, happy life" is popular for a reason. And so we see Paul exhorting Titus to invest in the women of the household of God so that they may be instructed with a healthy doctrine that bears fruit in their personal households. Why does Paul say that he wants the older women to teach the younger women about personal holiness and relational care in the home (Titus 2:3–5)? Well, he tells us why: "that the word of God may not be reviled" (v. 5). We see that this teaching that the older women are responsible to hand down must be handled with great maturity, because they are dealing with the truth of God's Word and applying it to people's lives, where it will bear fruit. And people are watching! Sisters, neighbors, wives, and mothers tend to be the cultivators in household relationships. We are gifted with a tenderness to loosen hardened egos, as well as a firm strength to destroy the weeds that may infect our families. Women have a way of multitasking these relational gifts in beautiful harmony when they are in accord with healthy doctrine. But our influence can be devastating to a family when we are self-serving and manipulative.

6. C. H. Spurgeon, *Autobiography*, vol. 2, *The Full Harvest* (repr., Edinburgh: Banner of Truth Trust, 1995), 442.

A woman's influence is not limited to her own home. Let's get back to the word *household* in our text in 2 Timothy. In their commentary, Bryan Chapell and Kent Hughes note, "The original Greek says '*the* homes.' They were probably the spacious homes of the wealthy, where house churches often met."[7] So it may be that these ungodly men are even more direct in using their stealthy tactics of manipulation by creeping into the house of God. These false teachers have a strategy. If they can deceive people with influence in God's household, they can cause the division and departure from God's Word that they are after. They are not just trying to deceive these women; they have the bigger goal of wreaking havoc in the whole household of God.

Opportunity

This term of contempt, "little women," reveals more about the women who were being manipulated. Robert W. Wall and Richard B. Steele explain in their commentary that this phrase, which they translate as "immature women," is "based on a common caricature of middle-class women in antiquity."[8] They explain that, unlike the working-class women, these were women with time on their hands. They had time to sit and listen to these impostors and then to spread this new teaching. Extra time is a blessing if it is stewarded well, but immature women do not use it for God's glory. Idleness provides a golden opportunity for someone who wants to introduce new doctrine into a church. These little women were convenient targets and tools to use in the spread of false teaching.

When we see this phrase, we are offended. It makes us

7. R. Kent Hughes and Bryan Chapell, *1–2 Timothy and Titus: To Guard the Deposit* (Wheaton, IL: Crossway, 2012), 245.

8. Robert W. Wall with Richard B. Steele, *1 and 2 Timothy and Titus* (Grand Rapids: Eerdmans, 2012), 262.

pause and consider whether we could be one of those women. But those who are "lovers of self . . . arrogant, abusive, . . . unholy, heartless," and seeking to take advantage of God's people, see an opportunity. In his epistle to the Ephesian Christians, Paul exhorts them, as they walk in the newness of their life in Christ, to put away falsehood (4:25). And so he warns them to "give no opportunity to the devil" (v. 27). There is a popular saying about how this happens: "Idle hands are the Devil's workshop." Idle people are inactive and lack purpose. But false teachers are highly active and purposeful. They are more than happy to give idle influencers-to-be something to talk about.

Susceptibility

Paul doesn't just use this term of contempt without qualifying it. If you combine idleness with being "burdened with sins and led astray by various passions, always learning and never able to arrive at a knowledge of the truth" (2 Tim. 3:6–7), you have some low-hanging fruit for the picking. Weak women are satisfied with half-truths because they are already invested in their sin. They are attracted to a counterfeit—to something that appears godly but doesn't embrace all of God's truth. When they don't trust God's Word to transform them, they deny its power. This is why Wall chose the word *immature* to describe "this working principle: these are female believers whose spiritual immaturity, not yet brought to maturity by the word of truth, are more easily seduced by false appearance."[9]

Why are we so insulted when we read this passage today? Because we should be! We don't want to be little women, immature in the faith, and an easy target for false teaching. Pastors, you wouldn't want such low-hanging fruit in your

9. Ibid.

church, would you? This text should shake us women up to evaluate our theological maturity and how that translates into our personal time, and it should shake the church up to evaluate how we are investing in women. Many of us, working class or not, have extra time on our hands. Are we using that time wisely? Or are we holding on to a particular sin that is weighing us down? The preacher to the Hebrews tells us to "lay aside every weight, and sin which clings so closely, and let us run with endurance the race that is set before us, looking to Jesus, the founder and perfecter of our faith" (12:1–2). If we are looking to Christ, to what he has done and what he is doing even now, sitting at the right hand of the Father and interceding on our behalf, then we are going to want to use our spare time to develop the spiritual stamina that we need to finish strong. That can translate into time in the Word, time in good fellowship, time serving our neighbors, and even some wholesome refreshment time to rejuvenate. Idleness is not to be confused with needed rest. But we can't forget that we are in a marathon of perseverance in the Christian life of faith and obedience.

Sin weighs us down and discourages us from our call to keep running. It also distracts us from the One we are to look to while running. That's when divergent teaching becomes appealing. Don't be susceptible! Make no mistake; weak women are still being targeted. Much of the material that is marketed to woman in the so-called Christian market is banking on our immaturity.

A Plea to the Officers of the Church

Now, how does Paul go about addressing this issue of little women and false teachers? Does he write, "Euodia, Syntyche, make sure that you study Romans before you read *Jesus Calling*?" No. He writes his warning to Timothy. Strange, isn't it? Paul is clearly addressing this as a problem in the church.[10] Pastors and elders, evaluate how your women's ministry is set up. What are the goals directing how it is organized? Are there some unintended opportunities for women who are burdened with sins to find respite in your women's groups? Do you know the resources that your women are using for teaching? Have you read them yourselves or looked into the authors? What is the goal for your women's ministry—or, if you do not have a formal women's ministry, for the women's Bible study or fellowship groups? Please, do not let your women be susceptible targets. This is a pastoral issue. Paul is writing to Timothy, who shoulders the burden for the integrity of his congregation.

Far too many motivated women are dealing with shallow women's studies—or, worse, just plain false teaching—in their church. One of their biggest laments is that the elders are unaware of the harm that these studies are inflicting on the women in their congregation. And the message from silence is that the women don't really matter. False teachers know how much women matter. Christian publishers know how much women matter as a target market. While the church, above all, knows that women are not tools for deception or a commodity for the market, it can sometimes be the very place where they feel undervalued in their most important role of all—as disciples of Christ. Initiative from the leadership in the church is needed to turn this situation around. Nothing will frustrate women more than to read this book and be left hanging in the breeze because their elders didn't bother to read it themselves.

No, not all women are gullible. But Wall and Steele are right: this is a haunting passage. We may think our desire to learn is a good thing in itself, but this passage shows us the danger of not coming to the knowledge of the truth. There are

---

10. Thanks to my pastor, Francis VanDelden, for these introductory sentences.

enemies making their way through the doors of our churches. These enemies may have some alluring things to say; they may even use some of our language. But where are they trying to lead God's people? They won't be satisfied with taking us just a little off track. Wall and Steele warn us that this situation is grave. These enemies are "further described as those who not only 'oppose the truth' and 'ruin the mind' but are without the intellectual equipment . . . needed to come to a knowledge of the truth and repent. Unlike that of Hymenaeus and Philetus, their situation is truly hopeless."[11] So it surely isn't harmless for women to learn from these unrepentant teachers who will ruin their minds.

The Good News

I'm not trying to beat everyone up with this warning (well, maybe a little). The only reason for me to write this book is that there's some great news to share. Paul writes his second epistle to Timothy in order to help instruct him to faithfully protect, preserve, and pass down what the apostles have delivered to the next generation. By the power of the Holy Spirit, Paul entrusts his missionary work at the church in Ephesus to Timothy, to "guard the good deposit entrusted to you" (1:14). While these false teachers are distorting God's Word, Paul encourages Timothy,

> But as for you, continue in what you have learned and have firmly believed, knowing from whom you learned it and how from childhood you have been acquainted with the sacred writings, which are able to make you wise for salvation through faith in Christ Jesus. (3:14–15)

11. Wall with Steele, *1 and 2 Timothy and Titus*, 263.

The "whom" used here is plural in its original Greek form. We see in the beginning of the letter that Timothy was brought up in the faith of his grandmother Lois and his mother Eunice (see 1:5).[12] So Paul is joining his own teaching to the teaching of these two important women in Timothy's life, with reference to how this pastor has been equipped to stand for God's truth.

You see, Paul does value the teaching of women. The good news is that Christ loves his church so much that he wants his entire household, including the women, to be able to teach and to help bring others to maturity. While they do not function in the office of a pastor or elder, women, like everyone else, are teachers. We should be good ones! And we see from Timothy's life that a mother and a grandmother can have great influence in the church. What if their theology had been weak? What if their guidance had been untrustworthy? Along with the laymen in the church, women help the pastoral ministry of the church as the preached Word of God works in us to "see to it that no one fails to obtain the grace of God" (Heb. 12:15). We look after one another in God's household.

The best news is that this good news flows from the work of Christ. We have all come up short in our learning and our teaching. I know I have embraced false ideas about who God is and what he has done when I have been weighted down with my own sin. I have squandered my privilege and responsibility before the Lord to bear his image and to glorify and rejoice in him. How are any of us worthy to call ourselves the bride of Christ? We are not, but for the love of Jesus, who fulfilled all righteousness on behalf of his beloved and took all our sin upon himself two thousand years ago. By faith we trust in his work to transform us into his own likeness as we strive to live a life of faith and obedience.

12. Note the significance in giving their names.

It is a privilege for us to learn about the great Bridegroom, Jesus Christ. It is a privilege to be called to worship in the household of God. But it is also an eternal matter. In his High Priestly Prayer, Jesus prayed, "And this is eternal life, that they know you, the only true God, and Jesus Christ whom you have sent" (John 17:3). Our theology, what we know to be true about God, is an eternal matter! Everyone in the church needs to be a good theologian. There will be no little women in the new heavens and the new earth. So what does that mean for the church now?

One of my favorite definitions, when I think about this, is, "Theology is the knowledge of how to live in the presence of God."[13] This is imperative for everyone to think about. We see how important this is in the very first chapters of Scripture. Gregory Beale contemplates this in one of his biblical theology lectures.

> How do we increase that presence [of God] in our lives, in our churches? How did Adam do it? I believe that after you believe in Christ that it's growing in the Word of God, ultimately, and obeying it. Remember what happened to Adam: he was sitting right there when Eve was misquoting Scripture. I already mentioned this early in the semester. She misquotes it in three different ways, and then she falls, and Adam falls with her. And I take it then that living in the light of God's Word is the way we live in the light of his presence. And if we don't live in the light of his Word, we're in darkness; we will fall; we will not have his presence. It's as simple as that, but maybe it's not real simple. It's not just

13. This is a rough translation that Timothy George offers from William Ames, *The Marrow of Sacred Divinity*, in his foreword to Gerald Hiestand and Todd Wilson, *The Pastor Theologian: Resurrecting an Ancient Vision* (Grand Rapids: Zondervan, 2015), 7.

reading the Word of God, but we have really got to have a mind-set to come to the Word of God and be willing to be transformed by it—not reading in our own thoughts, but praying that God's thoughts will form our thoughts, not that our thoughts will mold God's thoughts.[14]

Again, this is part of the good news. God has given us his Word, which is living and active by the power of his Spirit. He has given us everything that we need to live in his presence. Christians are new creations, justified by Christ, united to him by his Spirit, being transformed into his likeness and therefore prepared for glory. And so we see Paul encouraging Timothy to continue in the faith that he was taught by his teachers—Lois, Eunice, and Paul—with confidence that "All Scripture is breathed out by God and profitable for teaching, for reproof, for correction, and for training in righteousness, that the man of God may be complete, equipped for every good work" (2 Tim. 3:16). Now, as a pastor, Timothy has the special responsibility and privilege, in the ministry of Word and sacrament, to shepherd the people in the household of God to live in his presence, in light of his Word.

Nothing Less

The danger is to fall for a counterfeit. False teachers counterfeit the Word of God. They aim to deceive by imitating and distorting the truth. False teachers do this because it makes their message so attractive. But they want their thoughts to mold God's thoughts. Beale presses us to realize that it isn't

14. Gregory Beale, "A New Testament Biblical Theology: A Redemptive Historical Perspective of the Temple 1" lecture, Westminster Theological Seminary, Glenside, PA, mp3 download, 84:03, http://faculty.wts.edu/lectures/biblical-theology-a-redemptive-historical-perspective-of-the-temple-i/.

enough just to know God's Word, but that we must "pray that we're more willing than the demons" to follow it.[15] They believe and shudder (see James 2:19), yet they do not obey the Word and will not be transformed by it. Jonathan Edwards warns, "The devil is orthodox in his faith. He believes the true scheme of doctrine. He is no Deist, Socinian, Arian, Pelagian, or antinomian. The articles of his faith are all sound, and in them he is thoroughly established."[16] Knowledge of God's Word is not enough. We need to pray for God's thoughts to form our thoughts, and this takes conditioning in the Word of God and a willingness to live in the light of his presence.

Spirituality is a buzzword in our culture that has been horrifically overused. More and more people from different faiths and philosophies want to say they are spiritual. But what does that mean? We act according to what we believe to be true. Our spirituality is a living out of our doctrine. The Reformed church emphasizes in its doctrine of *sola Scriptura* that our spiritual lives flow out from submission to God's Word.[17] The Scriptures are our sole authority in matters of what we believe and of how we worship and live. And this cannot be an individual spirituality, because we see from Scripture that the church is the bride of Christ—those who tremble at God's Word (Isa. 66:2).

How does this work out between men and women in the church, wives and husbands, and church officers and laypeople? Beale is right; it isn't simple. The church needs to guard

---

15. Ibid.

16. Jonathan Edwards, *The True Believer: The Marks and Benefits of True Faith* (repr., Morgan, PA: Soli Deo Gloria Publications, 2001), 29.

17. Natalie Brand, *Complementarian Spirituality: Reformed Women and Union with Christ* (Eugene, OR: Wipf & Stock, 2013), 27. Brand defines Reformed spiritualities as "simply *manifestations of the same historical spiritual ancestry with its homogeneous traditional core values taken from the Reformation's recentralization of Scripture*" (pp. 27–28, emphasis in original).

its biblical truths and not settle for anything less. How can we sort through the heretical doctrines, theological errors, imprecisions, and in-house debates?[18] As we aim to live faithfully in the presence of God, embodying the mediation of Christ to the rest of the world, we can inadvertently allow false messages to slip into our own churches. While faithful churches subscribe to the scriptural basis for the ordination of certain qualified men to the ministry of Word and sacrament, it's easy to settle for something that sounds good—women's ministries—and to fail to evaluate whether its purpose and function are shaped by God's mission to his people.

Let's take a look at how easily this can happen.

Questions for Reflection and Discussion

1. Does your church have any type of mission statement for its women's initiatives? How does this mission statement, or lack thereof, affect women's influence both in the church and in their personal households? How can your church work to produce competent women, mature in the faith, who are able to teach what is good and are not susceptible to false teaching?

2. What do you think about John McKinley's translation of the word *ezer* as "necessary ally"? Does that affect the way that you think about women's ministries? How does this translation extend beyond the relationship between husband and wife? How is it broader than the typical categories of authority and submission that are associated with the translation "helper"?

3. Is there any idleness in your typical routine that could make you more susceptible to sin? Is there a particular

18. I will address those issues specifically in chapter 9.

sin that has been weighing you down and preventing you from persevering in your spiritual walk and in growing to maturity?

4. *Church officers,* here are the questions addressed to you specifically in this chapter: What are the goals directing how the women's initiatives in your church are organized? Are there some unintended opportunities for women who are burdened with sins to find respite in your women's groups? Do you know what resources your women are using for teaching? Have you read them yourself or looked into the authors? What is the vision for your women's ministry— or, if you do not have a formal women's ministry, for the women's Bible study or fellowship groups?

5. How do you understand the relationship between God's Word and your spiritual life? How would you say that the world outside the church defines spirituality? How is this a counterfeit for truly living in the presence of God?

ALWAYS LEARNING AND NEVER ABLE TO ARRIVE AT THE KNOWLEDGE OF THE TRUTH

We can read the account of Jesus with the woman at the well and find comfort that at least we're not as lost as she was, right? Now *there* was a little woman. She was outside the church. She was living in sin and didn't have a clue about true worship. Even so, we like to read the story, thankful that Christ cares about even the lowliest of the low, the Samaritans. We'd like to think that we would do the same. We'd like to think that we would be so generous with the gospel. But there's a lot we can learn from this account, even if we haven't had five husbands and don't wonder about which mountain to worship on.

In the biblical account, the bone-weary and thirsty Savior of the world doesn't travel around Samaria, as the Jews regularly did to avoid the Samaritans, but walks right on through it.[1]

---

1. This and the next four paragraphs are adapted from Aimee Byrd, "Always a Woman," *ByFaith*, April 11, 2016, http://byfaithonline.com/always-a-woman/.

And his disciples find that in his thirst he has plopped himself down to talk theology with a Samaritan woman. The Jews despised the Samaritans, looking down on them as idolatrous and unclean. What a sight for Christ's disciples to stumble upon as they are looking for their master! They dare not utter what has to be the obvious question as they approach a setting that is quite familiar to us, but is downright shocking to them.

"Why are you talking with her?"

It would have been a perfectly understandable question at that point in history. It was almost scandalous to think of the King of Kings drinking from the vessel of a Samaritan. And besides that, she was a woman! None of this made sense. Women were not considered worthy of theological discourse. It wasn't merely a question of how Jesus should invest his time with this woman. Rather, it was downright unsuitable, by conventional standards, for him to be seen chatting her up in the middle of the day at all.

So it is predictable that the disciples are silently wondering what the heck is going on. And yet, when John tells us that they didn't actually utter the question on their minds, we can imagine that the looks on their faces said it all.

How much of the conversation between Jesus and this woman did they hear as they were approaching? If they thought it was scandalous for the Savior of the world to be talking to a Samaritan woman in the middle of the day, the actual conversation that they were having would have been even more shocking. He was not just talking about the rest and water that his body needed. No, they were discussing the weighty matters of the gift of God, this woman's sin, right worship, and the coming of the Messiah. And then came the doozy. Just when the disciples approach, Jesus reveals himself to her, saying, "I who speak to you am he" (John 4:26–27). Nowhere in Scripture do we have Jesus revealing himself so clearly prior to his trial. We would expect to read about him saying this to someone like Peter or John. That's what the disciples would have expected too, right? But to a Samaritan woman?

This revelation changed everything for the Samaritan woman, who hastily dropped her water jar and ran to tell the whole town to come and see him. Many believed because of her testimony. But it wasn't her own words that she was seeking to share in a testimony. Her zeal wasn't to draw attention to herself. She led them to Christ, "and many more believed because of his word" (v. 41).

Let's back up and take a closer look at the interaction between Jesus and this Samaritan woman. Here she is, on a regular day, performing an ordinary routine of going to the well for water, and she runs into a Jew. Well, that isn't normal. And he has the audacity to ask her for a drink. Just as Paul uses the familiar term "little women" with Timothy to communicate contempt toward a certain type of women, this woman was well aware of the aversion that the Jews had toward Samaritans as a whole. John Calvin points out that her response was one of reproach: "How is it that you, a Jew, ask for a drink from me, a woman of Samaria?" (John 4:9). He comments that she may as well have said, "What? Is it lawful for you to ask drink from me when you hold us to be so profane?"[2] Here we have a woman admonishing true Goodness in a way that we ourselves are often not bold enough to confront *false* teachers! And yet the weary Jesus is persistent to pursue this woman. The man who asked her for a drink and was treated with disdain now offers her the gift of living water.

What a gift it is for us to have this account of Jesus resting by a well and then putting this woman's needs before

---

2. John Calvin, *Commentary on the Gospel According to John*, vol. 1, in *Harmony of Matthew, Mark, Luke, John 1–11*, trans. William Pringle, Calvin's Commentaries 17 (repr., Grand Rapids: Baker, 2003), 147.

his own. While he is physically exhausted, investing in this woman energizes Jesus. He even tells his disciples, "My food is to do the will of him who sent me and to accomplish his work" (v. 34). And so we have this recounting of Jesus talking about true satisfaction and true worship.

We may not be talking about mountains on which to worship, but true worship is a topic on the minds and hearts of many women today. And while the Samaritan woman isn't the same as the "little women" in the Ephesian church, we can see some similarities through this interaction. This woman's theology is an example of someone who is "always learning and never able to arrive at a knowledge of the truth." When Jesus makes the bold statement that if she knew the gift of God and who he is, she would be the one asking for living water, she pretty much comes back with a sarcastic, "Yeah, right!" Calvin picks apart her reply, "Are you greater than our father Jacob?" (v. 12), showing just how bad her theology was: "How faulty this comparison is, appears plainly enough from this consideration, that she compares the servant to the master, and a dead man to the living God; and yet how many in the present day fall into this very error?"[3]

She is so far from the truth that she can't recognize him standing right in front of her face! But don't we do the same thing when we have the whole Word of God before us and yet hold up someone else's teachings as having more authority?

We see, as the conversation continues, why this woman is learning without arriving at the truth. She is "burdened with sins and led astray by various passions." As a true teacher, Jesus confronts her with this after he reels her in. She challenges him to provide this living water that he is talking about, and he sets her up by saying, "Go, call your husband, and come here"

3. Ibid., 150.

(v. 16). And he doesn't accept the half-truth that she gives as her answer. Jesus then reveals to her that he knows the extent of her sin. This is when the conversation takes a turn. Now the woman knows her thirst, and her questions become more sincere. Acknowledging that Jesus must be a prophet, she asks about the right way to worship God.

Now that he has pointed out her sin, Jesus talks about worship in spirit and truth. There can't be true worship with unrepentant sin. Likewise, our selfish ambitions and false gods hinder our worship. We need to be called to repentance. And Jesus presses further on her bad theology: "You worship what you do not know" (v. 22). Think about the futility revealed in this sentence. She does not have the knowledge of the truth. Again, Calvin offers some pastoral counsel here: "Unless there be knowledge, it is not God that we worship, but a phantom or idol. All good intentions, as they are called, are struck by this sentence, as by a thunderbolt; for we learn from it, that men can do nothing but err, when they are guided by their own opinion without the word or command of God."[4]

This statement should undo us. Are people in our churches worshipping what they do not know? Tragically, many women full of good intentions are always learning and never able to arrive at the truth. Are we bold and compassionate enough to point that out?

The answer to the woman's question is Jesus himself. In him and him alone can she truly worship. And her response is to go out and bring others to Christ. The disciples could not have imagined the fruitful harvest they would reap from this one conversation that the weary and thirsty Jesus had with a Samaritan woman. They didn't even consider that the gospel would extend to Samaritans. Calvin rightly points out

4. Ibid., 159.

that, instead of being so surprised at the honor that Jesus had bestowed on the despised Samaritan woman, they should have been amazed at the honor he had given to *them* to be disciples of the Son of God.[5] Yes, Jesus Christ does love his church, his whole church, so much that he confronts the littlest of women, as well as those of us who think we are competent.

We Are Always Learning

The line in 2 Timothy about always learning is not used in a positive light. Like the Samaritan woman, we can be learning what is just plain false. Everyone is learning all the time. We learn when we have conversations, we learn while we are skimming social media, and we even learn when we are standing in the grocery store checkout line. Unfortunately, we are not always exposing ourselves to good teaching.

It can be especially encouraging for a pastor to have congregants who are intentional about what they are learning by being good readers. Having been through a rebellious several years in high school and in the beginning of college following my parents' divorce, and being absent from church throughout that time, I began wanting to learn more about my Christian faith by the time of my junior year. I had been partying it up a good bit and not living according to my profession of faith. This was a turning point for me, and for the first time I was making some social sacrifices for my faith. But, after I repented and turned back to the Lord, it became apparent that one doesn't just turn from a sinful outlook and behavior out of sheer willpower. What we believe to be true about God affects our behavior. I would need to learn more about the substance of my faith. If God's Word is true, as I was persuaded that it

5. Ibid., 166–67.

was, then I was responsible to learn from it. And it wasn't just going to be a decision to live better or not drink too much with my friends that was going to keep me going. I needed to have better desires. And that was beginning to happen.

I began attending a Sunday worship service at a local Baptist church. It was affiliated with the Southern Baptist Convention, which was the denomination I had grown up in. There are many fantastic Southern Baptist churches out there, but this one was not a hospitable one. The greeters were welcoming, even asking about where I was coming from. You would think that mentioning that I was new to the town as a student at the university would spark an invitation to a small group or a lunch to get me connected. But instead they would utter the "Isn't that nice" conversation ender. I don't remember much about the sermons, but I certainly wasn't part of the church community. I was just an individual attending a service and then returning to my off-campus living, left wondering what to do with this new resolve to take the whole Christian-living-in-the-world thing more seriously.

So I decided to turn in to the Christian bookstore that I had driven past on many occasions. That was my first time in a Christian bookstore, and it was overwhelming! I didn't know where to begin, but at least it seemed like a safe place to be. That's where I belonged, right? I was doing a good thing!

Stumbling upon a display near the front of the store featuring local authors, I found a book about living a Christian life that produces spiritual fruit. That looked like a topic worth learning more about, so I picked it up and immediately began reading. A likable, nurturing woman authored the book, sharing and teaching from her own experience. The most memorable part of the book was the introduction to a higher level of sanctification through speaking in tongues. I had heard about this before, but I thought it was for people on the fringes.

This kind, intelligent women linked my spiritual growth to communication with God through indecipherable language. Could it be?

Well, I figured, I had tried plenty of harmful things in my life, so I might as well give this supposedly godly practice a shot. So I went through all the motions of praying for the gift and then knelt there in my bedroom, mouth agape, waiting on my fruit . . . to no avail. Now a bit embarrassed, and certainly gaining a notch on my cynicism scale, I did learn something. I learned that there are different ways to teach from Scripture and that I didn't know much about the stances of other denominations—or even my own. While I didn't think that speaking in tongues was a common gift of the Spirit in our church age, I also didn't know the why behind it. And I didn't even know the biblical meaning of that gift in the early church. I realized that there was way more to this whole life of faith and obedience than a few minutes of quiet time a day. And that experience led me to the beautiful doctrine of the sufficiency of Scripture. But it took years of Scripture reading, theological maturing, trying to find a good church, and other sketchy encounters to get me there.

The Christian Danger Zone?
Pastors, Be Vigilant!

I'm sharing this embarrassing history to make a point. My story might sound funny, but it reveals something about Christian bookstores and the theological training of many of the women who walk into them. My first encounter with a Christian bookstore was before the days of massive Internet marketing and sales. So this isn't a problem that is going away, but one that is multiplying exponentially. Pastors need to be aware and up to date on the theology that women are being taught even in a so-called Christian context. Christian women's book studies have become quite popular, and many women in your church are also shopping for Christian books to read on their own. Because of this, Christian women have inevitably become a valued target market in the so-called Christian publishing industry. It is pumping out Bible studies, devotionals, customized Bibles, and personal growth books for us to buy (along with Christian candy, mugs, jewelry, and artwork). But the sad truth is that Christian bookstores can promote some of the worst doctrines (and their candy can be quite inferior). Just like any other market, we need to enter them with discernment. We do not want women's study groups in our churches to be promoting bad doctrine. They should be places where we can go for growth. Pastors, you don't want the women's studies in your churches to be potential danger zones. And women need to be encouraged not to check our discernment at the door.

This isn't a problem merely for college students who are just beginning to take their faith seriously (although that alone should motivate us!). Unfortunately, this is a problem even in confessional churches. I'm sure this is frustrating for pastors who labor in prayer and study to faithfully provide good preaching. What is the disconnect between sitting under the preached Word on Sunday morning and absorbing bad theology on Monday?

As women are sent out, aiming to live lives of faith and obedience in a post-Christian culture that can be hostile to our values, they are finding refuge and encouragement from engaging, thoughtful women authors and speakers who seem to be doing just that. I understand that it's hard enough to get congregants who like to read. And it must be encouraging when women are taking the initiative to grow in their knowledge of the Scriptures with further learning and study. But are they equipped to discern biblical truth from error? While good preaching is imperative for a healthy church, pastors are not only preachers; they are shepherds as well. Are church leaders in tune with the theological climate in their churches?

Many Christians do not distinguish between a likable personality and the content of that person's teaching. We are good at teaching our children that they need to look beyond personality when it comes to getting in a car with someone. We may teach our young ones that if anyone claims that we have sent them to pick them up, and if they haven't been notified first by us, then they must not get in the car no matter how nice the driver is. Or we may have an emergency family code word that indicates it is a person who they can trust. We warn our teenagers and young adults that even friends who they may normally hang out with are susceptible to making bad decisions with drinking and driving. No matter how much you like someone, it is never wise to let them drive under the influence! And under no circumstances should you get in the car with them.

Likewise, many of the women who teach troubling doctrines are very likable. Their books are well packaged, their talks are endearing, and they are exceptionally good at homing in on the common struggles that women are dealing with. They approach these topics with humor, self-disclosure, and warmth. And their lingo sounds pretty Christian. A woman from a big Baptist church, with a ministry called Proverbs 31 and a family that owns a Chick-fil-A and has adopted children from third-world countries, sounds pretty solid. Especially when she is offering to teach us wisdom for living, we think we can let our guard down.[6] People who have the same values

---

6. For my review, see Aimee Byrd, review of *The Best Yes: Making Wise Decisions in the Midst of Endless Demands*, by Lysa Terkeurst, Books at a Glance, February 4, 2015, http://booksataglance.com/book-reviews/the-best-yes-making-wise-decisions-in-the-midst-of-endless-demands-by-lysa-terkeurst.

as we do and who offer to teach us more about the faith are appealing, so we don't ask the critical questions about the content of their teaching. They look like fellow sheep who can help us with our everyday struggles.

But what gospel are they presenting? And how do they handle the Word of God in their teaching? This is where shepherding is needed. To be in tune with the theological climate of your church, you are going to have to be in tune with the theological climate of the evangelical subculture around it. What is being marketed and taught to your congregation under the guise of Christianity? This may sound overwhelming at first, so I want to help you. In fact, we are going to take a good look at this context in chapter 5, and this book closes with practical ways to learn how to read with discernment, along with some hands-on practice using excerpts from some of the best-selling books for Christian women. A vital skill for becoming a competent woman is learning how to read well. We need to be alert and equipped, because Christian bookstores don't have genre labels like "fluff" and "I may look like I have my life together more than you, but I'm about to wreck your theology."

You would be troubled to hear that women in your congregation were uncritically going on dates with random guys they had met, wouldn't you? What would you do in that situation? You would want to spend some time helping them distinguish between the attractive traits and the harmful ones. This is what we want to do with the books they are reading as well. There are practical ways to get help in developing a more theologically sharp congregation. Recruit members from your church who have a good grasp of the Christian book market and can inform you in this area. Find some websites and publications that offer trusted book reviews. This is a great opportunity to work with some of the discerning women in your congregation. You could enlist them to read a few popular books each year for review and discussion. And the discussion part is important. Setting up time to talk with the women in your congregation about what they are reading for personal growth and study is an act of good shepherding. Being involved in what materials they are using for teaching small groups is a responsibility of an overseer. You don't just want to provide a list of books that are dangerous for the women in your church to read, or throw a couple of book reviews at them. You want to build relationships, equipping women so that they know *how* to read. Hopefully chapter 8 will be a great tool to help you carry this out.

When Little Women Become Teachers

What if someone who is "always learning and never able to arrive at a knowledge of the truth" is teaching a women's study in the church? That wouldn't happen in a solid church, would it? Why is Paul so concerned about false teachers creeping into households and capturing little women? First of all, he doesn't want anyone in God's church to be infected by false teaching. But, as we saw earlier, women are influential in households. Maybe there weren't official women's studies going on in Timothy's church, but you can bet that these women were sharing false teaching at least in a casual fashion with those who would listen. And if this was a problem in the Ephesian church, it can easily be one in ours.

Pastors and discerning women have this very thing going on in their churches. Some of the churches that are the most protective of male ordination and authority in the church show little concern for what the women are studying. Often, in these situations, there is an undercurrent of manipulative women who are teaching other women doctrine that is subversive to the preaching from their own pulpits.

On the other hand, there are plenty of well-intended but unequipped women who are teaching from books that they found interesting in the Christian bookstore. Often the women's ministry is an entity of its own, left without much oversight from the elders. And so women who have all the appearances and intentions of upstanding church members, and who are gifted with the skill to teach, are given the freedom to lead a study. This is an unfair and unloving position to put them in without properly equipping and shepherding them.

Easily a whole chapter, or even a small book, could be filled with the stories I have heard about bad teaching in good churches. It is often difficult to have an edifying, civil conversation with those who insist on teaching material that is being questioned by a discerning and concerned church member or pastor. The pastor often looks like the bad guy if he comes in, after a study has already been established, to gently correct the teaching and offer something to replace it. Families begin to take sides, and some even leave the church. Women have approached their pastors or elders because their group is studying a book with false teaching, only to be ignored as if it doesn't matter because it's just the women's group. People have commented on articles I have written about nurturing theologically rich women's studies, saying that when they have pointed out quotations in their church magazine from mystics and other false teachers, their concerns have been dismissed by leaders in their church.

These are just a few examples of a very large problem. In one sense, we are always going to be up against bad teaching. But it doesn't have to be this prevalent in our small group studies and church reading material if we are investing in our leaders. And when error is detected, it is much better handled in the beginning, when the problem arises, than after your congregants become emotionally invested in a teacher or a particular author. Every congregant is responsible to be a discerning learner in the church, examining against Scripture the teaching that we receive (see Acts 17:11). And pastors and elders should exercise appropriate oversight of all the teaching going on in their churches.

Theology for Every Woman

Recently there has been more material addressing a topic that is relevant to the questions that women struggle with regarding their roles in the church, home, and society. In the last twenty-five years or so, the church has received some helpful teaching on biblical womanhood, and for that I am thankful. However, the church has also received some poor teaching in this area. And, while it is important to keep this conversation going, we may have unfortunately used the teaching of biblical womanhood as a filter through which we read Scripture and look at the culture. We now have niche devotional Bibles for women, entire parachurch organizations devoted to biblical womanhood, and many books tackling what our value and contributions are. So when it comes to women in the church, there's a temptation to narrow it down to what a woman can and can't do, what a woman can and can't say. We are getting the moral imperatives nailed down. But what I would like to do is to open up the doors of biblical womanhood and let the sunshine of theology for every woman shine through.

These are both exciting and confusing times for women. When my generation's grandparents were young women, the message was clear: get married, stay at home, and vacuum the house in your heels and pearls. Many of them passed on a very different message to their daughters: Don't stay isolated in your home! Get an education, pursue a career, have it all! And then there is my generation. We see that it is very difficult to combine June Cleaver with Hillary Clinton. And what about our daughters? Who are their role models, and what messages are they hearing?

All women wrestle with the good desire to contribute to both their homes and their communities, whether they are single, married, divorced, or widowed. But it isn't easy. What we may be missing isn't so much a better philosophy on home and work. What many of us need is better theology. No matter what our different circumstances and vocations may be, every woman is a theologian. We all have an understanding of who God is and what he has done. The question is whether or not our views are based on what he has revealed in his Word about himself.

And yet many women are either turned off or intimidated by doctrine. People often share that what is important is that we love God and love others, and that it just isn't necessary to get caught up in all that theological stuff. This kind of thinking is understandable. For one thing, theology can be intimidating. It's like when you go to the gym and hear the workout junkies talking about supination arm extensions and grasshopper push-ups. Suddenly you are feeling highly inadequate, unsure if you will ever have what it takes to be physically fit. Those people can be downright annoying, and so can some theologians. You may think you are having an edifying conversation about God, and then someone drops a bomb like "infralapsarianism." The next thing you know, you are part of a debate that you don't think really matters, involving terminology that is bordering on ridiculous. So, yes, theology can be intimidating. But we cannot let that stop us from pursuing it. So here are some reasons why theology is important for every person in the church, including the women.

Theology Is Confessional. It Unites and Separates.

In a closing statement on the Renewing Your Mind broadcast, Chris Larson states, "The future belongs to Christians of conviction."[7] Ligonier Ministries teamed up with LifeWay Research to conduct a survey of three thousand people in order to find out what Americans believe about God, the Bible, man, and salvation. The convictions of those interviewed in the survey are very bleak. Americans between the ages of eighteen and eighty-five and from different denominational backgrounds were asked to indicate how strongly they agree or disagree with statements like "There are many ways to get to heaven." Larson writes, "This study demonstrates the stunning gap in theological awareness throughout our nation, in our neighborhoods, and even in the seat next to us at church."[8]

The study seems to show that Americans have convictions about God, goodness, and even the afterlife, but not necessarily true, biblical ones. Seventy percent of churchgoers replied that they do not use historic creeds in their church. Stephen Nichols passionately points out how tragic that is: "That's just cutting yourself off from two thousand years of the Holy Spirit's ministry to the people of God."[9]

What are your convictions? Are they true? Does it matter? You may be reading this as an informed woman, mature in her theology. There is a survey available on the Ligonier website, provided in the footnotes on this page, where you can look at the theological questions that were asked. The results will reveal to you the state of theology in the church today. What can we do to improve this? The writer to the Hebrews emphatically exhorts us to persevere by holding fast to our confession of hope, as a covenant community, and to do it

7. R.C. Sproul and Stephen Nichols, "The State of Theology," *Renewing Your Mind*, Ligonier Ministries, podcast audio, October 28, 2014, http://renewingyourmind.org/broadcasts/2014/10/28/the-state-of-theology.

8. Chris Larson, "The State of Theology: New Findings on America's Spiritual Health," Ligonier Ministries, October 28, 2014, http://www.ligonier.org/blog/state-theology-new-findings-americas-theological-health/.

9. Sproul and Nichols, "The State of Theology."

without wavering (see Heb. 10:23). What is your confession? Is it the confession of hope, based on God's promises, that has been faithfully delivered in his Word and proclaimed by the church for two thousand years? Do we confess that Jesus is Lord? Who is Jesus, and what does it mean that he is Lord? Can you articulate this well to others?

The office of the pastor is important. He is proclaiming God's Word to his people in an authoritative way. The preached Word is a means of grace by which God's people are sanctified. What is the state of theology of American pastors? What would that survey look like? Probably a lot like this one. That is why it is so important for laypeople to understand their responsibility as theologians as well. That survey interviewed three thousand theologians, because all of us have some kind of knowledge about who God is. Many of them are terribly poor theologians. These results should be informative for pastors.

What is the state of theology? Every week we are called out from our ordinary work to gather together as a peculiar people: God's church. By grace, we are receivers of God's promised blessings in Christ, and we are sent back out with a benediction. A Christian without conviction should be an oxymoron. And yet we need to be warned to hold fast to our confession because there are many opposing forces. Our sinful natures are tempted to waver. We need theological stamina! We get that by actively engaging with God's Word, training ourselves by it, and exercising our faith. As Christians, we have been given a fighting faith to persevere.

Thankfully, we belong to a God who took an intra-Trinitarian oath before the beginning of time. As a result, he has entered into a covenant with his people to redeem and sanctify us through the blood of his only Son. And he who promised is faithful. Jesus is Lord, whether you confess it or not. Maybe you have cruised over to the Ligonier website and taken the survey for yourself, affirming that you know the right answers and that you are a good theologian. What is your witness? And what is our role in sharing our confession of hope?

The church has faithfully labored to preserve its orthodox profession of what a Christian believes. The historic creeds are gifts to us. We don't have to be overwhelmed when we go to God's Word, as if it just dropped from heaven to our generation, completely disconnected from history. Just as a map is helpful to a traveler, accurately depicting important roads and landmarks, creeds serve like maps to the Word of God, helping us to understand its teachings in a comprehensive way.

Our confession of hope is the good news of the gospel. We confess that Jesus is Lord. Carl Trueman elaborates: "Arguably, all of Christian theology is simply one long running commentary upon, or fleshing out of, this short, simple, ecstatic cry."[10]

Theology is confessional. And as our profession of faith unites us, we are separating ourselves from false teaching.

Theology Is Essential for Discipleship.

In the Great Commission, Jesus declares,

> All authority in heaven and on earth has been given to me. Go therefore and make disciples of all nations, baptizing them in the name of the Father and of the Son and of the Holy Spirit, teaching them to observe all that I have commanded you. And behold, I am with you always, to the end of the age. (Matt. 28:18–20)

Notice how much of his Word he commanded his apostles to teach: all of it!

---

10. Carl R. Trueman, *The Creedal Imperative* (Wheaton, IL: Crossway Books, 2012), 136.

Or think about Jesus approaching the two disciples on the road to Emmaus. Unable to recognize him, they share how distraught they are over the crucifixion and how confused they are by the latest news that the tomb of Jesus is empty and that he is alive. How does Jesus respond to them at this point? Does he comfort them, knowing that their intentions are good? No—he rebukes them for not knowing the Scriptures well enough and then gives them the sermon of a lifetime! Oh, how wonderful it would be to have that part of their conversation recorded, but I imagine it is similar to what we have in the sermon-letter to the Hebrews, showing us how all Scripture points to the ultimate Prophet, the ultimate Priest, and the ultimate King, Jesus Christ. Theology is essential for discipleship. If we are to be true disciples, we need to understand what the Bible says about Jesus.

Theology Requires Fitness.

The reason why so many people have an aversion to theology may be that it takes fitness. Returning to Hebrews 10:23, holding fast to anything requires fitness. It requires exercise, conditioning, and stamina. We are exhorted to hold fast to our confession of hope because there is always something working against our fight for spiritual health and growth. John Owen picks up on this, saying that these two words insinuate an opposing force—we could even say a "great danger." "To 'hold fast' implies the putting forth our utmost strength and endeavors in the defence of our profession, and a constant perseverance in so doing."[11] This is going to take awareness and a real fight. Faith is a gift of God, but it is a fighting grace. To be fit theologically, we must be conditioned by God's Word,

---

11. John Owen, *Epistle to the Hebrews*, abridged by M. J. Tyron (Grand Rapids: Kregel, 1968), 200.

exercising this gift *actively* by living a life of faith and obedience. As we strive to understand our confession of hope, we are emboldened to hold fast to it. God's Word and his promises should motivate us to live in a way that pleases him.

Relationships require the investment of our energies and time, don't they? Why would our relationship with God be any different? But the investment that we put into this relationship doesn't even compare to what he has already done for us. So we don't just want to learn information about God; we are invited into a relationship unlike any other. Thankfully, he is the initiator who knows us even better than we know ourselves. And he has graciously revealed himself to us.

Just as we may encounter that funny lingo at the gym, many of us find ourselves in specialized fields. If your doctor diagnoses you with Hashimoto's disease, you're not going to say, "Well that sounds too technical; I'm just not going to worry about it." No, you'll want to learn what the doctor is talking about. We trust doctors to listen to our symptoms in laymen's terms and then put them in the proper medical categories. If you had Hashimoto's disease, you would want to learn all that you could about it, including educating yourself on the doctor who gave you this diagnosis.

All of us have contracted a severe, fatal disease from sin. We see clearly in Paul's letter to the Ephesians that we are all born children of wrath (2:1–3). We would be hopelessly dead in sin were it not for the grace of God. But because of the work of Christ and the continuing work of his Spirit in application, he is bringing all those whom the Father has given him away from the reign of sin and death and into the reign of grace. And yet all of us who have received this saving grace are all too aware of our continuing struggle with sin. This is where the fitness comes in. We can read passages like Romans 6:5–11, about how our relationship to sin has changed now that we are

Christians. Twice in this passage, Paul appeals to knowing the work of Christ. James Montgomery Boice wrote in his commentary on this passage,

> A holy life comes from *knowing*—I stress that word—
> *knowing* that you can't go back, that you have died to sin and
> been made alive to God. Stott says, "A born again Christian
> should no more think of going back to the old life than an
> adult to his childhood, a married man to his bachelorhood,
> or a discharged prisoner to his prison cell."[12]

This is a positive exhortation for us to persevere in a holy life, holding fast to our confession of hope—our confession of what God has done and is doing. As the illustration in Hebrews shows us, it is like a marathon. We are going to need theological fitness.

Theology Is Practical and Necessary in the Christian Life.

What we know to be true about God shapes our everyday lives. Our conversion as new creations is only the beginning. We are being transformed into the likeness of Jesus Christ. So there should be no little women.

Unfortunately—and we'll see this more in chapter 6— much of what is marketed to women appeals to a desire to hear a special voice from God. Life is stressful. We have so many decisions to make that take wisdom and sometimes downright risk-taking faith. It would be wonderful to have direct revelation telling us the direction that God would have us take. But that is not the way he has ordained for us to grow.

12. James Montgomery Boice, *Romans* (Grand Rapids: Baker Books, 1992), 2:656, quoting John Stott, *Men Made New: An Exposition of Romans 6–8* (Grand Rapids: Baker, 1984), 51.

No, he wants us to count on the sufficiency of the Word that he has already given us and the wisdom to apply it rightly, in dependence on his Spirit. This is a lot more difficult. It requires prayer, discipline, reflection, seeking godly counsel, and stepping out in faith. But we are encouraged by the same words with which Paul encouraged Timothy:

> All Scripture is breathed out by God and profitable for teaching, for reproof, for correction, and for training in righteousness, that the man of God may be complete, equipped for every good work. (2 Tim. 3:16–17)

And that word "training" reminds us that we will be developing our fitness levels as we press on.

What is this life in which we begin to glorify God and enjoy him forever? Do we really believe God's Word, or are we looking to something else to find that joy when it comes to our everyday living? Theology is extremely practical. The study of who God is will direct our hearts to praise him and serve him in a life of faith and obedience.

Theology Is Covenantal.

We learn about the God who first loved us in the covenant community of his church. Christians are not meant to be individualistic theologians; we are part of the body of Christ. This is illustrated well throughout Scripture, but there are two little words in the sermon-letter to the Hebrews that stick out to me. After the greater portion of the sermon focuses on the indicatives on the person and work of Jesus Christ, there are three imperatives that we find in chapter 10, all beginning with "let us" (vv. 22–25). These are easy words to skip over. It is easy to read these imperatives as a command to individuals: "Hold fast your confession of hope without wavering." But that is not what Hebrews 10:23 says. It says, "Let *us* hold fast the confession of *our* hope." We hold fast to our confession of hope in the covenant community of the church.

And so the last of these three "let us" exhortations concludes,

> And let us consider how to stir up one another to love and good works, not neglecting to meet together, as is the habit of some, but encouraging one another, and all the more as you see the Day drawing near. (vv. 24–25)

The church is called to meet together. And specifically on the first day of every week, we are called out to join in corporate worship as the covenant community. Our text is God's very Word—a covenant treaty, of sorts, for his covenant people. Together we make up Christ's bride, for whom he will return. Christians are united to Christ, and we are to learn about our returning Bridegroom together, encouraging and exhorting one another as we wait for that day of consummation.

Women play a major role in the body of Christ and in showing the face of Christianity to the watching world. So we need to be well equipped with God's truth in our own lives. Of course, our gender does not affect the truth or who God is, but there are some nuances in the women's perspective and contribution that are different from those of the men. We also have some differences in our experiences and roles. This is why it is all the more imperative to share and communicate.

We are called to serve our churches and families as necessary allies—ones who sharpen the theology of others and maybe even challenge it sometimes. If women have a respectful attitude toward the officers in the church and the headship of their husbands, they are going to want to facilitate these roles by working alongside them as thinking women, fellow worshippers of God.

That is exactly what led me to be more serious in theological study. I recognize that I have an intuitive and relational disposition. I want my passions and gifts to be grounded in the truth. We don't need to fall into the traps of overgeneralizing or stereotyping the differences between men and women or of perpetuating the lie that women are designed to be man's exact clone. Our diversity as individuals reflects the beauty of God.

We can appreciate books that are written by women, for women, as long as they are biblically solid. And we will be getting into the nitty-gritty details of the good, the bad, and the ugly when it comes to these books later. But it can be helpful to learn with those who share similar experiences. And as we learn more about God, it's wonderful to have a group of women to discuss how theology applies in our specific roles. I'd love to see more women learning theology together. It is a great benefit to have like-minded women to encourage us in the gospel as we share both our successes and our failures in the Christian life.

We do have some wonderful resources for learning more about our roles as wives and mothers, as well as about topics such as homemaking and feminism. But there is more to a woman than women's issues, and we shouldn't limit ourselves to just those identities. Likewise, while we should glean from the profitable women's authors who write for us, we can also gain from reading male authors. With all the devotionals marketed to us, we may lose sight of the wonderful commentaries that are available for expositional Bible study. We don't need to limit ourselves to just living authors, either. We have a rich heritage of theologians who have proven their faith to the end, leaving behind treasures of writings. Systematic and biblical theology books, commentaries, and church history books are not just for seminary students and pastors. Ask your pastor or elders what may be some good resources for you to be a more well-rounded theologian.

As women learn together, we need to be intentional about coming to the knowledge of the truth. We must look at ways in which both church officers and the women in the church can plan for this better. We also need to learn from godly men. It is a blessing to be joined together in worship every Sunday and to sit under the preached Word as a covenant community. It is here, receiving this means of grace, that God promises to bless us in Christ. Let us not neglect that!

Questions for Reflection and Discussion

1. What books have you read in the last six months? What have you learned from them? Do you have some favorite authors or teachers? What attracts you to their writing and teaching? Which friends or family members do you learn the most from (this could be godly learning, or not so much!)?

2. Think about your everyday routines. What messages are you around? Do these messages sharpen you, challenge you, cause you to look to God's Word for wisdom, or tempt you—or do you feel ambivalent about them?

3. How well do you know the history of your own church and the denomination that it is affiliated with? If you belong to a nondenominational church, what is the history of its establishment, and what is its statement of faith? What is the extent of your knowledge of other Christian denominations and of some of the popular faiths that are not Christian?

4. *Church officers,* here are some of the questions addressed to you in this chapter: What are the top sellers in the Christian bookstore, and how faithful are they to God's Word? What is their appeal? Why would some of your congregants be attracted to their teaching? Are there any

people in your congregation who know the Christian market well and can help you in this area? Are you acquainted with some trusted websites and publications that you could refer to for book reviews? What if you were to ask some theologically sharp women in your church to read one or two books a year and review them? How can you help to ensure that the women in your church know its confessions and history better?

5. Sometimes we get so invested in our favorite authors and teachers that we have trouble separating their personalities from the content of their teaching. How do you handle it when your favorite books or speakers are challenged by constructive criticism? Do you take it personally? Do you think you have any blind spots when it comes to reading with discernment?

6. How can the women in your church uphold and promote the characteristics of theology taught in this chapter?

PART TWO

Examining Our Context

EVE, HOUSEHOLDS,
AND MARY

The first two chapters of the Bible tell us a lot. We've got a Creator God, a world, man, woman, beasts, birds and fish, gardening, fruit, culture, a kingdom, a priesthood, a mandate, nakedness, a covenant, a temple, marriage, provision, law, and goodness. Temple, garden, and household are woven together in one holy space that Adam and Eve are to expand. And their mandate gives them a joint mission to love God and each other. But love, even in the garden, has to be protected, because even there it comes under threat. If we read just the first two chapters, we don't know how all of the above is threatened. But only a couple of pages into Scripture we see it is threatened by bad theology.

The thing is, false teachers don't all hang out together in their own spaces labeled *Heretical Views* or *Bad Ideas*. No, they love to creep into places where discipleship is taking place. They want to make disciples for themselves. Well, where does discipleship take place? In the church! It's been that way from the beginning. The garden of Eden was a temple, a holy space, where God met with man. And we see some of that discipling in the first pages of Scripture.

We learn that God made man and woman in his own image, creating them male and female, and then gave them a mission: "Be fruitful and multiply and fill the earth and subdue it, and have dominion over the fish of the sea and over the birds of the heavens and over every living thing that moves on the earth" (Gen. 1:28).

Gregory Beale explains, "Humanity will fulfil the commission by means of being in God's image."[1] We see priestly language in the creation account, which says that man was put in the garden to "keep" it (Gen. 2:15), and we have the royal rule of dominion and subduing in the cultural mandate above. So as image-bearers, Adam and Eve have a mission. "God's ultimate goal in creation was to magnify his glory throughout the earth by means of his faithful image-bearers inhabiting the world in obedience to the divine mandate."[2] They were to expand the garden-temple, and therefore God's presence, to the outermost parts of the world.

It is additionally clear, from the union between Adam and Eve, that this garden-temple of Eden was also a household. And what was the overarching theme in their relationship? The text does not emphasize authority and submission, but unity in one flesh. This is not to say that Adam was not set as the head of the household, but the main point is unity. The church often misses this point, even with its good intentions, when trying to teach the distinctions between men and women. We even have the term *one flesh* to describe the union of Adam and Eve.

That unity is disrupted by the fall. And after the fall, we have the separation of the holy from the common. Woman

---

1. G. K. Beale, *The Temple and the Church's Mission* (Downers Grove, IL: IVP, 2004), 81.
2. Ibid., 82.

was created as a necessary ally of man, as we learned in chapter 1, but we quickly see Eve operating in antithesis to her design. She operates as man's opponent rather than his ally.

As the Serpent creeps into their household, Eve does not warn Adam to turn away from this evil. Rather, she is hospitable to the enemy, allowing the Serpent to converse with her in the garden-temple. While Eve seems to challenge Satan with God's words, she misquotes her Creator (see Gen. 3:3). Eve reads her own thoughts into what God said, instead of meditating on his word so that it really sinks in and shapes her. Therefore, rather than being a cobelligerent with Adam against evil enemies, properly meditating on God's word, and then giving wise counsel,[3] she participates in evil, speaks God's word falsely, and invites Adam to join her.

We're left to wonder: was Eve forgetful of God's exact words? And, if so, when does ignorance become rebellion? And that's the thing. Eve was responsible to know God's word and to handle it rightly (see 2 Tim. 2:15). I doubt that Eve was merely forgetful of God's exact words. Remember, before the fall, man's mind was not corrupted by sin. Adam and Eve didn't have faulty memories![4] In view of the instruction that God gave them in the cultural mandate, and the work of keeping, or guarding, the temple-garden that they were given as vice-regents, it would have been a rebellious act to be hospitable to a false teacher. God gave Adam and Eve what they needed to obey. So they can't be excused by innocent ignorance of his word or their vocation; instead, they are guilty of neglect and outright rebellion.

---

3. See John McKinley, "Necessary Allies: God as *Ezer*, Woman as *Ezer*," lecture, Hilton Atlanta, November 17, 2015, mp3 download, 38:35, http://www.wordmp3 .com/details.aspx?id=20759, for a discussion of how the things mentioned in this paragraph that Eve failed to do are in fact the functions of a necessary ally. These functions are also discussed further in chapter 7.

4. This is something I am really looking forward to in the new creation.

Furthermore, Eve had already begun exercising what she had been forbidden to do before eating the fruit. The tree of the knowledge of good and evil represents autonomy from God. It represents self-reliance and self-rule to determine what is good and evil. This is what Satan challenges. But man is not to determine goodness apart from what God, who is goodness, says! We are thoroughly dependent on God, and nothing is good outside of him. So, by entertaining this guest and keeping conversation going with him in the household-garden-temple of Eden, Eve is already practicing this autonomy. She is already beginning to turn from God. And Adam, who is with her, is doing the same.

Eve was not functioning as an ally to Adam but as his opponent. Instead of being a competent woman, she acted as a little woman. And together the first man and the first woman sinned against the holy God.

So Adam and Eve were expelled from the garden-temple. The temple, the home, and the civil community would thereafter be separate. This really complicates matters. Here we are, some two thousand years after the resurrection of Christ, and men and women are still trying to get a proper understanding of women in the church, in their personal households, and in society.

Household Missions and Household Codes

Interestingly, we see later in Scripture that the church is referred to as the household of God (see 1 Tim. 3:15). So there's still some connection between personal households and the household of the church. And, while certain cultural aspects of household codes and structures have changed over the years, there are some essentials that will carry over to the new heavens and the new earth. A household has a mission, and everyone belonging to the household is to be operating in furtherance of that mission. There needs to be some kind of order in a household for this to happen. Therefore, a household manager is needed to be responsible for the household's carrying out its mission.

In the beginning, the first household was given the mission of the cultural mandate. Adam and Eve were to expand the garden-temple-household, and therefore God's presence, throughout the earth. As the household manager, Adam was our federal representative. His obedience or rebellion represented all mankind. Eve was to function as his necessary ally in carrying out this mission. And in their marriage union, they operated in harmony as "one flesh."

Did the mission change after the fall? In God's grace, the mission did not change. We see it reestablished throughout the Old Testament and by Christ himself in the New Testament. But there is something interesting to note. Jesus gives the church the Great Commission to preach the gospel, make disciples, and administer the sacraments (see Matt. 28:18–20). This is a mission for the household of God. But all households are subject to the Great Commandment:

> You shall love the Lord your God with all your heart and with all your soul and with all your mind. This is the great and first commandment. And a second is like it: You shall love your neighbor as yourself. (Matt. 22:37–39)[5]

Of course, Christian homes will be functioning under both of these missions, with a better understanding of how they are connected.

5. Thanks to David VanDrunen for teaching this distinction so clearly in *Living in God's Two Kingdoms: A Biblical Vision for Christianity and Culture* (Wheaton, IL: Crossway, 2010).

There are two major sections of the New Testament that appeal to household codes, or patterns for family living. While many are quick to point out that Ephesians 5:22–6:9 and Colossians 3:18–4:1 are similar to the Greco-Roman household social structures, there is also a glaring difference. In the Greco-Roman structure, only the *paterfamilias*, the household manager, would be addressed with this kind of instruction. But these verses show women, children, and even household slaves directly addressed, because their service isn't first to the *paterfamilias* of their household but to God, the ultimate *paterfamilias*. They are reminded over and over again in the text that they are to fear the Lord, serve the Lord, and look to the Lord for their reward (Eph. 5:22, 24; 6:1, 5–9; Col. 3:18, 20, 22–24). Husbands are also instructed to serve the Lord and model the Lord in their love and service to the family.

The Household Manager

Biblical headship is not a micromanaging role but is one that trusts in and points to a greater household manager. Gregory Beale and Benjamin Gladd have done some great work, on Christ as household manager and on how that connects to the first married couple, in their book *Hidden But Now Revealed*. They have a chapter dealing with the use of the word *mystery* in Ephesians, in which they begin with the claim, "Paul casts his net wide in Ephesians 1 and then tightens it as he progresses through the letter."[6] As the net is cast wide in the beginning of the epistle, Ephesians 1:3–14, the authors home in on verses 9–10 (NASB): "He made known to us the mystery of His will, according to His kind intention which

---

6. G. K. Beale and Benjamin L. Gladd, *Hidden But Now Revealed: A Biblical Theology of Mystery* (Downers Grove, IL: IVP Academic, 2014), 148.

He purposed in Him with a view to an administration suitable to the fullness of the times, that is, the summing up of all things in Christ, things in the heavens and things on the earth." Of course, this word *mystery* should cause us to wonder what new thing has been revealed. And the terminology in this verse invokes household language. The authors explain, "The mystery has to do with Christ overseeing a 'household management' (or 'administration,' *oikonomia*) of the 'fullness of times' that refers to the latter days (Eph. 1:10a)." This household management is part of the revealed mystery, "the summing up of all things in Christ, things in the heavens and things on the earth."[7]

The first Adam wreaked havoc on God's "cosmic household." Since sin has entered the world, the mission of God has been challenged, and we lack love for God and one another. That's actually an understatement. Paul explains in this epistle that we were once children of wrath, dead in our sins (see 2:1). So we didn't just lack love. Without Christ, we are haters of God, enslaved to sin. Jesus, the second Adam,

> came as a household manager to put God's cosmic household back into order. The main focus of the revelation of the mystery is that Christ is the point of reintegration and restoration of the original cosmic unity and harmony that had been lost at the fall of humanity, a fragmentation that had affected not only earthly but also the heavenly realm.[8]

Just before Paul "tightens" his net, revealing that he is talking about a profound mystery, he quotes from Genesis 2:24: "Therefore a man shall leave his father and mother and

7. Ibid., 150.
8. Ibid., 151 (emphasis in original).

hold fast to his wife, and the two shall become one flesh" (Eph. 5:31). It's significant that he does this within his teaching on household codes. Beale and Gladd make the connection between this first marital union and the household codes for the "new creational community. The household code is intimately bound up with the gospel and believer's relationship to it (Eph. 5:1–21)." What does Adam and Eve's marital union have to do with the gospel and our households now? And what is this household management dynamic in the fullness of time? "In addition to restoring people groups in the cosmic household, Christ has come also to put back together the fragmented relationships of individual family households: husbands and wives, parents and children, and slaves and masters."[9]

In these household code verses in Ephesians 5, we have responsibilities laid out for the wife and the husband with reference to the first couple in Genesis 2:24. "The logic of Genesis 2:23–24 is the following: woman is man's intimate partner and companion, so much so that they are a unity (Gen. 2:23); therefore . . . , marriage is the ultimate expression of this creational relationship (Gen. 2:24)."[10]

This is interesting, because we know that in the new heavens and the new earth, we will not marry or be given in marriage (see Matt. 22:30). The church is the bride of Christ, and we wait for the consummation on that great day of his return. Christ is the ultimate household manager, *paterfamilias*, to which any other head points. Will men be less manly in the resurrection because they will not be the head of a woman? Of course not! And what leadership roles will we be given in God's consummated household, where temple, garden, city,

9. Ibid., 174.
10. Ibid., 175.

and home are once again united in holiness? I do not know. But something that Hannah Anderson has said in her book *Made for More* is important as we are preparing for that day: "When we craft our learning and discipleship programs around being 'women,' we make womanhood the central focus of our pursuit of knowledge instead of Christ."[11] When we look at the structure of households, in both our families and the church, the main focus should be our mission. We serve in that mission as men and women, and it is important to understand how we relate and work together biblically. But we do that best with our central focus in mind.

Beale and Gladd reveal the significance of this passage in Genesis within the context of mystery and household codes. *"Genesis 2:24 is the fountainhead of Israel's conception of marriage and serves as the paradigmatic expression of marriage,"*[12] and that is then metaphorically applied to God and his dealing with Israel in the Old Testament (Isa. 61:10; 62:2–5; Ezra 10:1–4), including God's end-time marriage relationship with Israel in the latter days. Ephesians 5 then applies the Lord's relationship with Israel to Christ's relationship with the church. *"Christ becomes identified with the Lord and the church is identified with the true end-time Israel."*[13] So Adam and Eve's union in marriage *"typologically corresponds to Christ and the church."*[14] This profound mystery has now been revealed.

The social order or chaos within a household, both in Bible times and to this very day, is a witness to those on the outside. The Greco-Roman household code contained both essential aspects of a household that would endure and cultural

---

11. Hannah Anderson, *Made for More: An Invitation to Live in God's Image* (Chicago: Moody, 2014), 105.
12. Beale and Gladd, *Hidden But Now Revealed*, 175 (emphasis in original).
13. Ibid., 180 (emphasis in original).
14. Ibid., 181 (emphasis in original).

structures that would ebb. Paul's teaching on marriage within this code of proper relationships between the members of the family promotes social order and places that under the umbrella of the mystery revealed in Ephesians 1:10, of Christ overseeing a household management.

So we see that Christ, as household manager, is working in both God's household and family households as he is summing up all things. So what is it that the head of a household does here in these last days? And when we are talking about elders in God's household and husbands in family households, what is their responsibility in exercising authority and leadership?

Oikonomos Theou

Let's go back to Paul's first epistle to Timothy to look at this household analogy more closely. He opens up his letter:

> As I urged you when I was going to Macedonia, remain at Ephesus so that you may charge certain persons not to teach any different doctrine, nor to devote themselves to myths and endless genealogies, which promote speculations rather than the stewardship from God that is by faith. The aim of our charge is love that issues from a pure heart and a good conscience and a sincere faith. (1 Tim. 1:3–5)

The English translation here doesn't really capture the household theme that is present in these verses. The phrase "stewardship from God" translates the Greek *oikonomos theou*, which Robert Wall better translates in his commentary on the Pastoral Epistles as "God's way of ordering the world." He explains that Paul is referring to what we may even think of as mundane tasks in managing a household. Wall notes a similar phrase in Titus 1:7, *theou oikonomos*, where Paul is speaking of "the congregation's . . . 'administrator' (see 1 Tim. 3:1–7)." Similarly, Paul uses the term "in Gal. 4:1–2 of the heir's relationship to his 'trustees' . . . as analogical of Christian conversion."[15] He continues,

> The catchphrase *oikonomia theou* is probably rooted in this same typological soil and envisages a kind of divine trusteeship by which the triune God manages the outworking of salvation's history within the ongoing community of faith. . . .
>
> Moreover the letter's wide-ranging instructions are formative of the church's existence in the world as God's household, and as such make it a public microcosm of the *oikonomia theou*.[16]

We see important pillars for this stewardship in 1 Timothy 3:1–7, where we have the qualifications for overseers, or "household administrators," with God as the head of his household (v. 15). Wall points out how this household metaphor is predominant in the Pastoral Epistles and that God's way of ordering the world (see 1 Tim. 1:4) is what should be taught in the church, over against the false teaching combating it. If a member could not manage his own household well, he certainly was not going to do well as an overseer in God's sacred household (3:5). Wall continues,

> Those in charge of caring for the family household, from its administrator to its servant staff, had particular responsibilities and observed particular social conventions. The stability of the city-state, if not of the empire, was routinely considered by its politicians and philosophers to be dependent

15. Robert W. Wall with Richard B. Steele, *1 and 2 Timothy and Titus* (Grand Rapids: Eerdmans, 2012), 65.
16. Ibid.

on maintaining its various households. While the vocation of God's sacred household is religious, its daily operations require effective administrators and a competent servant staff, like any other Roman household.[17]

A few verses later, in 1 Timothy 3:14–15, Paul continues on this theme.

> I hope to come to you soon, but I am writing these things to you so that, if I delay, you may know how one ought to behave in the household of God, which is the church of the living God, a pillar and buttress of the truth.

Wall focuses in on this theme of the *oikonomia theou* in the Pastoral Epistles, showing that our relationships within our families and in the household of God bear witness to God's mission to the world.

With that in mind, let's tie this household language in with Genesis 2:24. As God is putting his household in order, we have a beautiful eschatological picture in marriage. In the last lecture of his biblical theology series, Beale points out that every time a man leaves his father's household to cling to his wife (Gen. 2:24), we have "a parable, a repeated parable, of what Christ would do as the husband of the church: leave his father, cleave to the church. He would initiate as the . . . preserver and leader, and be the instigator and source of unity and nourishment, and the church should respond in trust." He continues that, when a husband lavishly and sacrificially gives to his wife, providing her with what she desires (as long as it is not sinful), he is showing the fallen world something about what Christ has come to do. And when a wife is able to

17. Ibid., 99–100.

offer and does offer trust to her husband, the watching world is shocked by our "walking lifestyle of the gospel."[18]

You see, there is a theological mission connected to being the head of a household. Going back to the practical questions, what exactly is the responsibility of a head? Wall again sheds light here, emphasizing that it is a responsibility to tend to the mission and purpose of the household. Our mission is to be summed up in Christ's household, to be sanctified for his purposes, and to reign with him in the new heavens and the new earth. This eschatological goal shapes the mission of the household. This mission needs to reach the next generation and the ones after that. And so the head of the household needs to ensure that the household's faith is articulated well, that the members of the household live according to that faith, and that it is passed down to the next generation. This is true both of the family and of the household of God—his church.

And so Wall explains how this leadership plays out. Leaders "think about the mission, describe it, communicate it, keep it constantly before the group, and develop goals on the basis of it."[19] If only Adam would have done that! Because there is always great opposition to the mission, these household-themed exhortations always come alongside warnings about false teachers. Wall interestingly points out something that Paul makes clear in the opening to his first letter to Timothy: "While love is the moral aim of the *oikonomia theou* and is spiritually adduced (1:5), it is threatened not by misbehavior but by bad theology."[20]

We don't bear witness to God's mission to the world by micromanaging male/female relationships, regulating the

---

18. Gregory Beale, "A New Testament Biblical Theology: The Eschatological Role of the Holy Spirit II," lecture, Westminster Theological Seminary, Glenside, PA, mp3 download, 72:14, http://faculty.wts.edu/lectures/biblical-theology-the-eschatological-role-of-the-holy-spirit-i/.

19. Wall with Steele, *1 and 2 Timothy and Titus*, 259.

20. Ibid., 171.

details of femininity and masculinity when it comes to serving in our vocations, or insisting on some kind of blanket male authority over all women in society. It is a lot more nuanced than "men can do this, and women can do that." And women are not merely sidekicks in male vocations. We love our neighbors in service together, as men and women. And we promote God's mission to the world by functioning in our households as God has called us to. And what a great privilege that is!

When a Good Teacher Walks into Your House

The account of Jesus visiting Martha and Mary in Luke 10:38–42 is a redemptive contrast to Eve and the Serpent. Here we have a good teacher—no, the Good Teacher—approaching a household. Martha is always looked at as the bad guy in this story, but she does something wonderful. Unlike Eve, Martha is hospitable to the good teacher. Jesus doesn't creep into her household, either. Martha invites him.

In the very next sentence, we learn that Martha has a sister, Mary, and that she "sat at the Lord's feet and listened to his teaching" (v. 39). How long did Mary sit there listening to Jesus before Martha spoke up? I've been on the fuming end, serving in the kitchen and feeling left with the chores while everyone else is having all the fun. First I think, "Oh, so-and-so will notice that I could use a hand in a few minutes and jump in." And if that doesn't happen, some extra clanging of the dishes will not so subtly get my point across. Martha may have used a tactic like that and then checked to notice Mary still sitting there, looking even more enthralled by what Jesus was saying. I can imagine Martha wanting to be there too but thinking that she was doing the more admirable thing. After all, she invited him in, and she wanted to be a good hostess.

Who knows how long Mary was sitting there learning before Martha finally spoke up: "Hey, remember *me*? . . . Jesus, you're the Good Teacher; remind Mary how this whole household code thing works!"

But we know that he doesn't. And let me state the obvious: women love this verse! Many of us are "anxious and troubled about many things," and for good reason. It takes a lot of work to keep a household going. Just the other day, my friend Jim posted this on Facebook: "It is amazing how much time and energy must be focused each day by at least one member of a household in order to meet the continuing sustenance needs of the whole." Truth! The fact is that people need to eat, sleep, and live in cleanliness and good order so that they can function properly in their relationships and vocations. And that takes a lot of work! But there is something, one thing, that is necessary, and Mary identified it.

This is crucial for women to know in order to function properly in their design as necessary allies. We are first disciples of the Lord. This is where Eve failed. Eve was hospitable to God's enemy, allowed God's word to be challenged by him, and in turn revealed her own lack of attention to it. Here we have Mary treasuring God's word and the presence of the Lord in her home. Eve wanted to recognize good and evil on her own, so she ate the fruit of the forbidden tree, the one forbidden by the source of Good. Mary sat at the feet of Good and fed on his word. She sat to learn, openly, when she had other responsibilities, knowing that she was leaving Martha hanging and was drawing attention to herself. Who did she think she was? But that isn't even the question. Jesus showed Martha, and us, that it's about who *he* is. This completely reorients our thinking.

It's interesting that their brother, Lazarus, is not mentioned in this account. These three siblings had a special relationship with Jesus, but we are first introduced to the women.

We see neither of them in the role of a wife, mother, or daughter—not even in the role that we know they have of being sisters to Lazarus—in this first recorded account of their relationship with Jesus. Mary is introduced to us as a disciple of Christ, "which will not be taken away from her" (v. 42), and Martha is invited in as well. Jesus is talking theology with two women, and that is their most important role. It will affect everything else that they do. And some of that is shared with us later in Scripture.

Later, when their brother is deathly ill, they know they need Jesus. And when he finally arrives, after Lazarus has been dead in the tomb for four days, Martha is the eager one this time who goes out to meet him. And she makes some profound theological statements. It's a confrontational conversation. Martha tells Jesus that if only he would have been there earlier, her brother would still be alive. She's basically saying, "I know what you can do, but you didn't show." Jesus responds, "Your brother will rise again." And Martha retorts that, sure, she knows her eschatology—her brother will rise again in the resurrection on the last day. And then, once again to a woman, Jesus reveals himself: "I am the resurrection and the life," whereupon he declares the gospel: "Whoever believes in me, though he die, yet shall he live, and everyone who lives and believes in me shall never die." As if this isn't powerful and gracious enough, his next words turn the tables on Martha: "Do you believe this?" It's not about Lazarus. It's not about Martha. It's not about when Jesus should have arrived. It's about who he is! And Martha responds, "Yes, Lord; I believe that you are the Christ, the Son of God, who is coming into the world."[21]

It's interesting how similar her answer is to Peter's confession of who Jesus is (see Mark 8:29). She identified Christ,

21. See John 11:23–27.

invited him into her home, and was transformed. Women do
not always need to be busy with other things; they need to
know who to listen to. Jesus does not treat Martha, Mary, or
any other woman as the intellectually inferior sex. We see in
this relationship a woman who *learns*. She engages. And she
learns straight from the source, not through another man—
such as her brother or a husband—as a mediator.

Now Jesus calls for a chance to talk to Mary before entering the house. This time, Mary falls at the feet of Jesus. And
she opens with the same line as her sister. We read that Jesus is
deeply moved, or indignant, when he sees her weeping along
with the Jews who have followed her for consolation. And
when they lead him to Lazarus, he weeps too. There's dis-
agreement on whether Jesus wept out of compassion for Mary,
because of the sorrow of death and the curse from sin, or over
the fact that these people whom he loved still didn't get it—
who he is! But this is the only family in Scripture whom we
see him weeping with. And he shows them the glory of God
by raising their brother from the dead.

In one more account, Jesus shows up dining with these
three siblings. Mary does another shocker. She takes almost
twelve ounces of expensive perfume and anoints the Lord's
head and feet with it.[22] This time, it's not Martha who wants
Jesus to rebuke her, but Judas Iscariot, followed by the other
disciples. You see, Martha has learned as his disciple. She knows
who he is. And by this amazing act, one that Jesus says will
be remembered forever when we speak of the gospel, Mary
shows that she has been listening to the Lord's teaching. She
also knows him. She understands his person and work. In fact,
his other disciples could learn from her. Jesus shares that Mary
is preparing him for his burial. But earlier, when Jesus foretold

22. See Matthew 26:6–13; Mark 14:3–9; John 12:1–8.

his death, Peter rebuked him in disbelief! We see Mary submitting to what is about to happen, and Jesus calls this one-time act beautiful. Calvin reflects on the prophetic nature of this act, "since Christ, in departing from the sepulchre, perfumed not one house, but the whole world, by the quickening odour of his death."[23]

A Message to the Household Stewards

If you were to ask both the men and the women about the culture in your church, do you think they would give the same answer? I've heard that men tend to answer the question about how their marriages are progressing more positively than women do. Is that also true in the church? In some ways, not serving as elders or pastors, women can be protected from some of the uglier issues in a church. But you don't want the men leading and serving as elders to foster an exclusively male culture in God's household. As we consider our mission, being prepared for the new heavens and the new earth as new creations and expanding God's presence through his spiritual kingdom now, how does it affect the relationships in the church between men and women? Are all the good friends of your church's officers men? Of course, we need to have maturity and discernment so that we are not crossing any boundaries. But Jesus was close to Mary and Martha. It was important for him not only to equip them well as disciples but also to cry with them. He wasn't just a teacher; he was a friend.

We all know that pastors and elders need to be very careful, as Satan would love nothing more than to bring church leaders down with sexual scandal. We shouldn't

23. John Calvin, *Commentary on a Harmony of the Evangelists, Matthew, Mark, and Luke,* vol. 3, in *Harmony of Matthew, Mark, Luke, John 1–11,* trans. William Pringle, Calvin's Commentaries 17 (repr., Grand Rapids: Baker, 2003), 191.

underestimate that concern. And you're not Jesus, so you don't need to have the women falling at your feet or anointing them with perfume and wiping them with their hair. But let me write to you as a woman who loves the church and who has been in a faithful marriage for nineteen years. Sometimes women can get the message that their sexuality makes them some sort of disease to be avoided by good men in the church. And so sometimes it seems that the worse of two evils is picked. In order to protect themselves from the temptation or appearance of sexual impropriety, many pastors and elders keep their relationships with all women at acquaintance levels. While it is loving to have boundaries in place, you don't want to miss out on good friendships. And we can build healthy friendships within appropriate boundaries that are proper for married people. Our pastors and elders have the opportunity to model what we are being prepared for as brothers and sisters serving together in the new heavens and the new earth. We need to learn more than what *not* to do. We need to learn what *to* do—not only in our marriages, but in our friendships as well. As a matter of fact, that's what all of God's people should be learning well, from the children to the youth group and all the way up to the seniors. Then we can better serve together in carrying out and passing on our household mission with joy.

Members of a household benefit from and treasure the relationships between the sexes. Your church is God's household. Many of the people in it build friendships with their neighbors, their classmates, and their coworkers. Is it less taboo to have healthy friendships with the opposite sex in secular society than it is within the church? I hope not. Healthy relationships grow out of serving together. This is what we want for God's people. Are you looking at the women in your church as necessary allies of the household?

Hospitality within God's Mission

This chapter opened with a hospitality no-no: entertaining the teaching of a creeper. That's what the little women who Paul mentions in 2 Timothy were doing, and that was Eve's deadly mistake. Satan showed up at the metaphorical door as the craftiest beast, and Eve basically said, "Come on in." Adam, who knew his mission to work and to guard the garden-temple—which is a priestly job[24]—was there with her, not protecting the temple from the enemy. Hospitality is not always a good thing. John warns,

> If anyone comes to you and does not bring this teaching, do not receive him into your house or give him any greeting, for whoever greets him takes part in his wicked works. (2 John 10–11)

He is referring to the teaching of Christ (v. 9). So our hospitality needs to be informed by the teaching of Christ.

It's interesting that John addresses his second epistle to "the elect lady and her children" (v. 1). Who is that? Well, we have good reason to think that he is referring to the church, since we are the bride of Christ. But while there are Scripture verses in which the church is given a feminine pronoun, this specific term is not used elsewhere. So some think that this letter is addressed to a literal woman. We don't know for sure. The closing, "The children of your elect sister greet you" (v. 13), adds to the plausibility of John addressing a church. What a great name for the church! This was a time of the traveling evangelist teacher, a time without church buildings and Holiday Inn Expresses. God's messengers of the gospel

---

24. See Num. 3:38; 8:26; 18:5.

depended on good people for hospitality. But the elect lady needs to be focused on the mission. Our acts of hospitality need to be theologically cognizant.

False teachers are still knocking on the door. Boy, do they love to get in the church! Paul alerts us to this over and over again in Scripture. This admonition in Romans 16:17–18 sounds a lot like what he wrote to Timothy:

> I appeal to you, brothers, to watch out for those who cause divisions and create obstacles contrary to the doctrine that you have been taught; avoid them. For such persons do not serve our Lord Christ, but their own appetites, and by smooth talk and flattery they deceive the hearts of the naive.

Our evangelical culture is one that promotes tolerance and love. But it isn't loving to tolerate bad teaching in the church. Love requires the work of guarding the Word of the One who truly is loving. He loves us enough to be direct about holiness, sin, and the way to everlasting life. We have a responsibility to discern the teaching of those who eagerly wish to disciple others. And this includes the books that we use in the church.

My aim in this chapter has been to get us thinking more about the household structure of the church. This is important as we think about the contributions that women make to the household and the reasons for appointed household managers. Headship is connected to household, and this is because a household has a mission that needs to be carried out in proper order. In a household that is set up properly, women should thrive alongside the men as they serve according to their giftedness and the needs of the church.

Hospitality is a major part of our mission, both within the church and as a means of evangelism and loving our neighbors. The gospel is to be shared with everyone, but its message is

also to be guarded. All members of a household share responsibilities here. As Paul says, "The aim of our charge is love that
issues from a pure heart and a good conscience and a sincere
faith" (1 Tim. 1:5). But he warns us against false teaching and
bad theology. He tells us to hold fast to the faith, to healthy
doctrine, "in accordance with the gospel of the glory of the
blessed God with which I have been entrusted" (v. 11).

Martha and Mary recognize the real thing when they see
it. Jesus himself invested in them as disciples. This is what
we want for all women in the church. We want them to
know the most important thing, "the good portion." So what
does that look like in our churches now? After all, many
churches have ministries dedicated to women. Let's take a
more critical look at women's ministries with this household
mission in mind.

Questions for Reflection and Discussion

1. Read Genesis 1:26–31; 2:10–3:7. How did Eve's mishandling of God's word reveal her bad theology regarding
   the character of God? What kind of God does the Serpent
   suggest they have? And what do God's words in Genesis
   1:29–30 reveal about his generosity and love?
2. What would a household be like without a mission? Have
   you ever been in a household that lacked management, or
   one in which the management was not supported but was
   sabotaged instead? How would it affect a personal household and its mission if only one spouse were a Christian?
3. How is the church a microcosm, or a little picture, of the
   stewardship from God (i.e., God's way of doing things)?
   Does this change the way that you think about worship,
   service, and relationships in his household? What impact
   does this make on your roles in your personal household?

4. What is the important connection between the household-themed exhortations in Scripture and the warnings about false teachers that we find beside them? How is love threatened by bad theology?

5. While we know that Christ, our *paterfamilias*, should always be our focus in everything we do, we are easily distracted by other things as we serve in our many roles. What tends to distract you the most? What gets you really upset or provokes you to lose sight of the mission and to turn on those you are to serve alongside in your own household, instead of working together?

6. *Church officers*, here are some of the questions addressed to you in this chapter: If you were to ask both the men and the women to describe the culture in your church, do you think they would give the same answer? As we consider our mission, being prepared for the new heavens and the new earth as new creations and expanding God's presence through his spiritual kingdom now, how does it affect our relationships in the church between men and women? Are all of your good friends men? Are you looking at the women in your church as necessary allies of the household?

7. How is hospitality connected to God's mission? Why is it so important for us to be good theologians when it comes to hospitality?

8. If headship is connected to household management, are all men to have authority over all women? And what are the responsibilities of the heads of households?

HOW THE CHURCH
MINISTERS TO
EVERY MEMBER

I am a woman who is a Christian and who loves to be a part of women's Bible studies. I used to think that this meant I should be actively involved in a women's ministry. But I haven't always been sure what women's ministry should entail. And one theological concern that has been nagging away at me is the use of this word *ministry*.

It seems that everyone in the church needs to be a part of some kind of niche ministry these days, and women's ministry is the queen of them all. As Protestants, we believe that Jesus is our only mediator between believers and God and that by grace we are all gifted with his Holy Spirit. And, since Scripture tells us that each Christian is given spiritual gifts for use in serving Christ's body, we have developed a popular manner of thinking about every-member ministry.

It's a simple matter of stewarding our gifts, right? So now we talk about my ministry and your ministry, Randy's ministry and women's ministry. With all this excitement over serving with our gifts, we may have lost sight of the value of *the* ministry.

The ministry of the Word and sacrament, administered by particular people who are ordained in the office of ministry, is the gift from God by which we are all blessed. Michael Horton has written on the topic of every-member ministry in a helpful way in a few places. In *The Christian Faith*, he critiques some of the newer translations' handling of Ephesians 4:11–12, such as the ESV's "And he gave the apostles, the prophets, the evangelists, the shepherds and teachers, to equip the saints for the work of ministry, for building up the body of Christ," saying that older translations, such as the KJV, may have a better grasp of the meaning of the original text. The KJV reads, "And he gave some, apostles; and some, prophets; and some, evangelists; and some, pastors and teachers; for the perfecting of the saints, for the work of the ministry, for the edifying of the body of Christ." Do you see the difference between the two? Horton points out,

> Reflecting the actual construction of the Greek, the older translation draws three lines of purpose clauses from the offices given that newer translations obscure. The same officers who are given for the completion (not equipping) of the saints are also given for the work of ministry and edification of the body. On this reading, Christ has given apostles, prophets, evangelists, and pastors and teachers for the ministry of the Word that brings the whole body to unity, maturity, and completion in the truth. This is not to say that the body is complete in and through these offices alone, for there are other gifts mentioned elsewhere (esp. Ro 12 and 1Co 12). However, the focus here is restricted to that work of bringing unity and maturity to the body through sound doctrine.[1]

1. Michael Horton, *The Christian Faith: A Systematic Theology for Pilgrims on the*

Horton also notes that this text in Ephesians differs from the other two major passages of Scripture dealing with the spiritual gifts, Romans 12:3–8 and 1 Corinthians 12:4–28, which include gifts such as service, generous giving, acts of mercy, hospitality, and administration. It's only in the Ephesians passage that we see the explanation that Christ, in his ascension, gave the officers of his church as a gift for the purpose of building it up "until we all attain to the unity of the faith and of the knowledge of the Son of God" (Eph. 4:13). Sure, Christ is generous to give us all spiritual gifts with which we serve the church, but that isn't the point of this passage. Paul gets to that, beginning in verse 17, but first he shows the priority of the ministry of the Word. This ministry is a gift to his bride! And Paul explains that this will help the church, pictured as Christ's body here, to grow in unity, protected from false teaching and building itself up in love (vv. 12–16). Horton continues,

> Before they serve, they are served. This underscores again the remarkable generosity of the church's victorious head, that he would make his people receivers first and active givers as a result.
>
> While every member and every gift is needed in order for the body to be fully operative, the very life of the body depends on the faithful maintenance of the ministry of Word and sacrament.[2]

We downplay the value of this amazing gift, and our need for it, when we call all our less formal programs and services *ministries*. Christ, the head, ministers to every member through Word and sacrament: women, men, marrieds, singles, elderly,

---

Way (Grand Rapids: Zondervan, 2011), 887–88.
2. Ibid., 888.

and children. It's not that we shouldn't have any initiatives for these groups, but if every way in which we serve others with our gifts is called a ministry, then the gift that we so desperately need ourselves—the ministry of Word and sacrament—blends in to look like just another ministry among many. And it is easy to become so wrapped up in *our* ministering that we lose perspective. Ministry can easily slip into a man-centered agenda that we pursue for our own ambitions.

Women are ministered to by Word and sacrament, just like everybody else. That is the formal ministry of the church. Just as there isn't a special Bible for women and a special Bible for men, both men and women are built up together through the ministry of the Word. Danger creeps in more easily when we begin thinking of ourselves as having a ministerial status. This may not be our intent when we talk about informal ministries, but, as Carl Trueman has said, we downplay *the* ministry of Word and sacrament when we hijack the word *ministry*.[3]

These are the main reasons why it's not helpful to use the term *women's ministry*. When we talk about *the* ministry, there is clarity about what it entails: particular people, particular means, and particular results. In the ministry, we have the officers of the church serving in God's household through Word and sacrament, for the maturity and unity of the faith and of the knowledge of the Son of God. One thing that has always confused me about women's ministry, no matter what church I've been to or what books I have read, is what exactly it entails. Is it a ministry to women or by women? What are the particular means for carrying out this ministry? And what results are we hoping to achieve?

---

3. Carl Trueman, "Bannerman Take Two: When the Levy Breaks," *Postcards from Palookaville* (blog), Alliance of Confessing Evangelicals, April 17, 2015, http://www.alliancenet.org/mos/postcards-from-palookaville/bannerman-take-two-when-the-levy-breaks#.Vng8VDaYfwx.

What Comes under the Umbrella of Women's Ministries?

Christ has given the church the gift of ordained ministerial office, and that is how the church ministers to every member through Word and sacrament. With that in mind, let's look at how this relates to women's ministries. What comes under the umbrella of women's ministries?

For many churches, women's ministry includes hospitality services such as organizing and making meals for new moms or someone who is ill, inviting visitors over for coffee, baby showers, and perhaps even organizing the Sunday morning greeters. These are wonderful services for a church to provide, but why is hospitality put under the umbrella of women's ministry? The biblical command to be hospitable is not directed only at women.

Despite their best intentions of having a thriving women's ministry that serves the church well, the men themselves may be missing out on the blessings of serving in some of these areas that are designated for women. We may be divvying up services between men and women unnecessarily and thus missing opportunities to serve together.

Gender distinctiveness is a major cultural challenge that the church is up against in our day. It's real and good, and yet how do we express it? Women's ministry can sometimes add to this problem rather than help it. How can we display gender distinctiveness and exemplify healthy male-female relationships in the church as brothers and sisters in the Lord? How do we model the hope that we have for living in the new heavens and the new earth as new creations while living in the already and the not yet?

We can add to this problem when all the ways that women serve in the church are isolated in a women's ministry. And, as we've already seen, we lose our focus on *the* ministry that we all truly need. Women's ministry is not an office of the church. Here's the thing: complementary churches may be paying lip service to the importance of male leadership in the office of pastor and elder, while simultaneously neutering them in their ministerial role. We recognize that women are gifted in many ways to serve and teach, and we think that we create a safe place for them to do that by offering women's ministry. These often informal and organically formed groups become viewed as the place where the real ministry is happening because of its practical value. And then we say we are being complementary because we have designated a separate wing for women to do their thing in the church. It has the appearance of valuing women and giving them a place to serve under male headship, but far too often these women are not properly invested in by that headship or led in the most meaningful way.

So it's easy to see how women's ministries can have problems with some version of the little women warned against in 2 Timothy 3:6, who get caught up in false teaching and can infect a whole church. This is ironic, since most women's ministries begin as an attempt to apply one of the "pinkest"[4] passages in Scripture. You know what I am talking about. You can't discuss women's ministries without discussing Titus 2. Here we see a call for the mature women to be teaching the younger women of the faith "what is good" (v. 3). This verse recognizes that women teach women all the time, whether they are equipped to do it or not. Remember, *little women* is a term of contempt for a particular group of women. They have time on their hands. They are easily seduced by teaching that

---

4. I first encountered this term in Hannah Anderson, *Made for More: An Invitation to Live in God's Image* (Chicago: Moody, 2014).

has an appearance of godliness but lacks the real thing. This is happening on a major scale in the church today.

Churches can have great teaching from the pulpit on Sunday, and yet different teaching may be let in throughout the week. Where is the discernment? What are we missing? Maybe it has become easier for false teachers to target little women to infect the church because we have separated them in their own ministry. There are so many books full of bad theology that have been written with women's groups in mind. Pastors can hardly keep up with what women are up against in the danger zone labeled "Christian publishing." But it is imperative that they do. With the technology that we have today, not only do false teachers have more access to spread their doctrine, but the weak people who they target move on to start their own blogs, publish their own books, speak to their own crowds, and lure in more of the same.

We are all familiar with Titus 2. But we forget whom it is addressed to. Paul is instructing Titus as he is bringing his ministry in Crete to a close and equipping elders there to carry on the work they have begun. Some of his main concerns are the organization of the church and dealing with false teachers. We see in this letter how the ministry produces fruit in all the different people in the church. Titus is exhorted to teach sound doctrine (see v. 1), and then, under his ministerial care, mature women are to "teach what is good" (v. 3) to younger women in the faith. We see in these verses how doctrine and life go hand in hand, and mature women should not only model this but also train the younger women. This isn't a mere appearance of godliness but an embracing of sound doctrine and of its fruit.

The elders have a responsibility to invest in the women so that they are equipped to teach what is good. Women teaching women flows from the ministry. What we do in our own households flows out from and pictures our participation in the household of God.

I'm all for having the women of the church plan fellowship activities together. In fact, I love being a part of that. I especially love attending women's retreats and conferences that are full of good teaching. It's been an honor to do some speaking to various women's groups. I have learned from many of the women at these retreats, and they have been a great blessing to me.

Of course, we should be encouraged to use our gifts to serve the body of Christ and show love to our neighbors. However, do we really need a formal women's ministry to organize this? What we do need is to prioritize the ministerial office given to the church and its role in equipping lay members in teaching what is good. Our service and conversations are shaped by the theology that we believe. Let's be passionate about investing in good teaching and in the discernment needed to spot counterfeits. Let's improve communication between the leaders in the church and the women who teach so that they can lead solid women's Bible studies and book studies that are developed from the ministry of Word and sacrament. This will be a blessing to the elders and to the church as a whole.

What Makes the Church the Church?

"Many, perhaps indeed most, of the controversies which have arisen in connection with ecclesiastical theology, are to be traced back to fundamental differences of opinion regarding the essential nature and character of that society which Christ has instituted."[5] We use the word *church* all the time, and it

5. James Bannerman, *The Church of Christ*, rev. ed. (Carlisle, PA: Banner of Truth, 2015), 5.

can have all kinds of meanings. In its broadest definition, we talk about the invisible church, which consists of all believers united to Christ our head, including those who are now with the Lord in heaven.[6] But even when we talk about the invisible church, Roman Catholics have a different definition than Protestants do. Catholics give priority to the visible church, making the invisible church subordinate to it and especially to the authority of its magisterium. Rather than an inward working of the Spirit with the Word, producing faith and repentance, the priests of the Roman Church deem a Christian to be a member of the visible church, making outward sacrifices and obtaining "outward cleansing by penance and absolution."[7] Protestants, on the other hand, profess that "the primary and leading idea of the Church is unquestionably the Church invisible, comprising the whole body of the elect, for whose sake a visible Church has been established on this earth at all."[8] This important distinction properly acknowledges the authority and work of God as the head of his church.

Although this is not typical, some people are in the invisible church but are not part of the visible church community, whether as a result of extenuating circumstances, deathbed conversions, or other reasons unknown to us. And there are those who are members of visible churches, even active members, who are not genuine believers and therefore are not united to Christ in the invisible church. Even ordained officers of the church do not have the power to infallibly discern who is in the invisible church or to "give birth"[9] to it. This blessed privilege is "according to the purpose of [God's] will, to the praise of his glorious grace, with which he has blessed us in

---

6. See the Westminster Confession of Faith (WCF) 25.1.
7. Bannerman, *The Church of Christ*, 41.
8. Ibid.
9. Ibid., 40.

the Beloved" (Eph. 1:5–6). It is God who makes the church the church. Period.

And even when we begin talking about the visible church there are some distinctions. In the New Testament, we see the visible church as "an outward society formed upon the inward and spiritual one, and established and maintained in the world for its benefit."[10] But this definition can then be narrowed down to a particular denomination (with its confessional, governmental, and worship distinctives), one or more regional bodies, and finally the local church that you attend, "represented by [its] office bearers and rulers."[11] And this is the part we will focus on as we talk about the church. It's important for us to take ecclesiology seriously when we are talking about ministry in the local church.

Distinguishing the role of the office-bearers and rulers of the church does not downplay the priesthood of all believers and our common privileges and responsibilities when it comes to the stewardship of our gifts in love and service to one another. It's the gift that God gave to his church so that we can thrive in carrying out his mission. All believers, who were once enemies of God, enslaved to their own sin, are equal recipients of God's saving grace. Herman Bavinck states,

> Objectively, that grace with all its benefits appeared in Christ, who acquired and distributes them in the way of the covenant. The fellowship of those who have received Christ with all his benefits is called "the church" or "the Christian community." *How does Christ communicate his benefits to his people, to the church? Does he use means?*[12]

10. Ibid., 15.
11. Ibid., 16.
12. Herman Bavinck, *Reformed Dogmatics*, abridged ed., ed. John Bolt (Grand Rapids: Baker Academic, 2011), 643 (emphasis in original).

Of course he does! Scripture makes this clear. And we see in Ephesians 4 that this is Christ's gift to his church.

The Ministerial Office

"The responsibility of teaching the truth of the gospel is given to all believers in their various places and callings, but in an official way through the teaching of the minister of the Word. The office does not suppress the gifts, but, rather, only guides them."[13] The teaching office of the ordained minister is set apart from other teachers in the church, for their benefit. We see some of the practical significance of this office in the Pastoral Epistles as well as in the emphasis that Paul gives to its priority and continuation. For example, he charges Timothy to "entrust" what he has learned from Paul in the "presence of many witnesses . . . to faithful men, who will be able to teach others also" (2 Tim. 2:2). James Bannerman makes some points from this verse that are worth sharing. He says that it implies two categories: the "*teachers* and the *taught* . . . the one being a special and peculiar office in the Church, and not the common calling of all its members."[14] He then points out an important word in this text. The qualifications of faithfulness and ability to teach are what I notice, but Bannerman points out that there is another important qualification in this text, which is the word "commit," as it reads in the King James Version that he uses, or "entrust," as we have it in the English Standard Version. This shows the necessity for an "authoritative commission entrusted to them," and thus the "*committal* of the work to them by Timothy."[15]

Just a few verses before that one, Paul refers to the gift of

13. Ibid., 633.
14. Bannerman, *Church of Christ*, 490.
15. Ibid., 491 (emphasis in original).

God given to Timothy, "which is in you through the laying on of my hands" (1:6), followed by the charge to "guard the good deposit entrusted to you" (v. 14). So this "presence of many witnesses" in 2 Timothy 2:2 is likely referring to Timothy's ordination. He is to guard the deposit entrusted to him, and he has the responsibility and authority to entrust that to other qualified men.

This leads us to ask where this kind of authority comes from. Does this ministerial office originate with Paul and then pass to Timothy, and then from Timothy to whomever he sees fit? "Is the office itself of human or Divine origin?"[16] We are talking about God's household here, not any common institution. And when Christ gave the Great Commission to make disciples, baptizing and teaching them, he made it with a promise that he would be with them. Let's look at that more closely. First Jesus said, "All authority in heaven and on earth has been given to me" (Matt. 28:18). Christ is the one with all authority over his church (and over the whole heavens and earth!). With that authority, he commissions his disciples to expand his spiritual kingdom by bringing those whom he calls into the ministry of the visible church "in the name of the Father and of the Son and of the Holy Spirit" (v. 19). They are to teach not their own doctrines, but all that Christ has commanded them. They are ministering and baptizing in the name of the Father, the Son, and the Holy Spirit. And then comes the promise: "And behold, I am with you always, to the end of the age" (v. 20).

From this verse, Bannerman infers that "the office of teaching and administering the Sacraments was to be perpetual and permanent in the Church."[17] Christ is carrying out this mission to the end of the age. Also, these verses reveal that the ministerial

16. Ibid., 445.
17. Ibid., 447.

office in this age originated as a divine appointment. We see both the human ministry of the disciples and the "agency of the Spirit to be present with them and make them effectual."[18] This is a holy office, set apart for the mission of God's spiritual kingdom. Christ is the head of his church, and this is the way he has set up his church as *the* household manager.

This is an office that we should respect—one that we do not want to subvert or make light of by viewing it as merely one ministry among many. And yet it should go without saying that our ministers are not pointing to themselves but pointing to Christ through his Word, the authority for us all. And, by means of the ministry, they confer Christ and all his blessings on the church.

To the Ministerial Officers of the Church

While your office is unique among the gifts in the church, you know all too well that each part of the body needs to be working properly in order to carry out God's mission. As you deliver the means of grace of Word and sacrament, you continue to shepherd the flock to build up the body of Christ. Of course you want to make sure that the youth, the women, the men, the seniors, and any other group are reached. There is a sense in which we could say that your ministry trickles down to something that may be called the women's ministry. At least the usual intention for all the ministries in a church is that they would flow from *the* ministry. Ultimately, all of God's people are called to "see to it that no one fails to obtain the grace of God" (Heb. 12:15). This is a call for all members to have oversight over one another as brothers and sisters in God's household, promoting one another's holiness.

18. Ibid.

But is using the term *ministry* for all our areas of service the most helpful way to identify how groups and individuals in your church are nurtured in the Word and called out to serve one another? When we hear that someone is in the office of the ministry, we know that there was an important process involved to equip him for his shepherding vocation. To distinguish the office of the ministry from the ministries in the church, some choose to refer to a "capital *M*" ministry and "lowercase *m*" ministries. Couldn't we use a better label, like *women's initiatives*, to describe the aim of your own pastoral ministry? Maybe some of you don't have niche ministries in your church for this very reason. *Women's initiatives* isn't a term that I have come up with but is one that I have heard used and taken notice of. Using a term like this makes a statement that the ministry of Word and sacrament is distinguished. Calling something a ministry can give the appearance of an individual or group's already having been equipped with the qualifications to carry out an office. But the term *initiatives* implies a purpose of growth toward a certain goal. This way, the leaders of the church can add clarity to the mission of these initiatives, investing in groups for their members' growth in sanctification as well as structuring these initiatives as outflows of *the* ministry.

It also indicates that these groups are part of a bigger whole. Women's ministries often function as their own separate entity. We will get into this in the next chapter, but there are women's ministries that are not affiliated with a particular church at all. But having women's initiatives in your church can make it much clearer that they are functioning as an outflow of the ministry of Word and sacrament and not as an independent mission. This would also remind the officers of the church of their responsibility to continually shepherd and invest in this group. I like that a lot!

You may perceive some teaching and leadership gifts in a particular woman and think that you have your leader for a women's group. Maybe there are several women in your church whom you can identify as having the maturity, charisma, and gifts that would make a good leader. And with all the resources available for topical and Bible studies for women, things may seem lined up pretty well for a women's ministry. So you ask these women if they would be interested in leading, and you let them work out the details. Now all you need are some intriguing pictures of these women in action for your website and you are good to go.

Okay, that last sentence sounded smarmy—but I wanted to pack a couple of rocks in my snowballs for extra effect. Women's initiatives are important. All the women need investing in, so why not begin by investing in the leaders? If there is a clear mission for the women's initiatives in your church, then the officers of the church should have a plan for equipping qualified women's leaders. You will want to help develop their teaching gifts, and you will want to make sure that they have good resources for learning, preparing lessons, and teaching the women in your church according to the ministry already given to them by Christ.

The women's initiative would not just function as a group in and of itself, to be served and to serve its own pet causes. There's nothing wrong with pet causes, and as we are sent out with a benediction every Sunday, we will all have some. But initiatives will aim to build relationships within the church between all its members. They will also help the officers of the church to be more intentional in their relationships with their sisters in Christ. Who do you surround yourself with? Jesus and the apostles, including Paul, had women in their inner circles. And it wasn't just a strategy to "reach the women" and use their feminine appeal to their own kind. These women were helpful to them as friends. Look, your elders are in the innermost circle of church government, and hopefully at least some of them will even be your close friends. But this whole enterprise isn't just about government. We are talking about a household. We are talking about community, familial community. This leads to my last point.

Women Are Necessary Allies to the Ministry

This chapter began with the question of how the church ministers to every member. While it's imperative to uphold the main work of the ministry of Word and sacrament, that doesn't mean that women, and in fact all lay members, don't contribute to and participate within this ministry. While we do have male leadership in the ministerial office, we don't want to promote a male culture in the church. Women are not only necessary allies to their husbands within their personal households but are also necessary allies to the men in carrying out the mission of the household of God. And in this way, women have distinct and diverse contributions to make alongside their brothers in Christ.

Christ's own ministry involved women as necessary allies. The women who followed him while he was "proclaiming and bringing the good news of the kingdom of God" (Luke 8:1) played an important role in his ministry. Mary Magdalene, out of whom Jesus had previously cast seven demons, was among the women mentioned as traveling with him and financially supporting his mission. That's right, we have many women mentioned as providers for the ministry. This is downright scandalous, according to some of the teaching today about "biblical womanhood." Yes, I did—I just used the words *women* and *providers* in the same sentence! The wife of

Herod's household manager is mentioned specifically, along with a woman named Susannah, about whom we are told nothing else in Scripture. Luke mentions that these women and "many others" were "healed of evil spirits and infirmities." Here we have a diverse group of women represented by three specific people: one who was probably a social outcast, one who must have left the comforts of the upper class to follow Jesus, and one who was probably more like most of us: an ordinary woman whose life was changed forever by the Son of God (see Luke 8:1–3).

After all the disciples had deserted Jesus, and even after Peter had denied him three times, Mary Magdalene is specifically mentioned again among the many women who were witnesses of the crucifixion. These women had "followed Jesus from Galilee, ministering to him" (Matt. 27:55). While it clearly wasn't *their* ministry, we do not want to overlook the fact that these women were able to minister to Jesus under his ministry. They were his allies in the mission—to the end! The disciples fled in fear, but these women remained faithfully nearby. While men are the ones typically thought of as strong enough to deal with gore and tragedy, we see "many women" who are the ones with the inner strength and resolve to witness the crucifixion without turning away from their beloved Savior. They remained there while the land was completely dark, from the sixth to the ninth hour—three hours in darkness! They remained there while the Son of God was mocked and given sour wine. Oh the horror of what they saw! The giver of life was struggling for his next breath. The one who had healed them and discipled them cried out to his Father in heaven, "My God, my God, why have you forsaken me?" They remained there while he gave up his spirit. And they were there when "the curtain of the temple was torn in two, from top to bottom. And the earth shook, and the rocks were split."

They remained there while "the tombs also were opened. And many bodies of the saints who had fallen asleep were raised." They remained there while the centurion and others who were there exclaimed, "Truly this was the Son of God!"[19]

How do Matthew, Mark, and Luke know these details? Because, by God's providence, these women remained there, despite the horrors that they saw, and then gave witness to these crucial events in the glorious gospel that we share! John did not flee, but Calvin points out how these women are the ones mentioned, "deserv[ing] preference above the men," which "suggests a severe reproof of the apostles. . . . Accordingly, when they afterwards proclaimed the gospel, they must have borrowed from *women* the chief portion of the history."[20] These women indeed served as necessary allies with great fortitude.

The gospels then teach us that it was the women who took care to return to the tomb of Jesus with spices and ointments and who discovered the stone rolled away and no Jesus inside the tomb. Instead, there were two angels who shared the wondrous news that he had risen from the dead! Also, it was Mary Magdalene to whom Jesus first appeared in his resurrected body. She got the honor and privilege of sharing this news!

And again, immediately after the ascension, Luke records that these women accompanied the disciples, along with "Mary the mother of Jesus, and his brothers," to pray before the outpouring of his Holy Spirit (see Acts 1:12–14). Women were an active part of the work of *Christ's* ministry, not of women's ministry. Don't misread my upholding of the distinct office of the ministry of Word and sacrament as saying that women

19. See Matthew 27:45–56; see also Mark 15:40–41; Luke 23:44–49.

20. John Calvin, *Commentary on a Harmony of the Evangelists, Matthew, Mark, and Luke*, vol. 3, in *Harmony of Matthew, Mark, Luke, John 1–11*, trans. William Pringle, Calvin's Commentaries 17 (repr., Grand Rapids: Baker, 2003), 329 (emphasis in original).

should not be actively involved in the ministry. In fact, we are necessary allies to the ministry, and separating ourselves in our own "ministries" can detract from this.

As the early church was being established, women continued to function as necessary allies. As Paul is closing out his letter to the Romans and getting more personal, he commends the person who would deliver the epistle to them: "our sister Phoebe, a servant of the church at Cenchreae, that you may welcome her in the Lord in a way worthy of the saints, and help her in whatever she may need from you, for she has been a patron of many and of myself as well" (Rom. 16:1–2).

This is a loaded commendation! First of all, let's just think of the work of delivering this letter to the church in Rome. Donald Grey Barnhouse writes, "Never was there a greater burden carried by such tender hands. The theological history of the church through the centuries was in the manuscript which she brought with her. The Reformation was in that baggage. The blessing of multitudes in our day was carried in those parchments."[21] Again we see a woman sharing profound theology with God's people. James Montgomery Boice points out that most likely Phoebe had others traveling with her, given the unsafe conditions for women to travel alone in the ancient world, which makes it all the more significant that she is the prominent one delivering the epistle.[22] Phoebe was probably simultaneously traveling for business of some sort, which is why Paul also told the church in Rome to help her in any way that she might need it during her stay.

Phoebe has stirred up some debate that still continues in

---

21. Donald Grey Barnhouse, *God's Glory: Exposition of Bible Doctrines, Taking the Epistle to the Romans as a Point of Departure*, vol. 10, *Romans 14:13–16:27* (Grand Rapids: Eerdmans, 1964), 124, quoted in James Montgomery Boice, *Romans* (Grand Rapids: Baker, 1995), 4:1913.
22. Boice, *Romans*, 4:1913.

the church today. The Greek word that we see translated as "servant" is the word used for *deacon*. Was Phoebe a deaconess? Many believe so, while many others would say that that isn't the case. This text alone does not answer the question one way or the other. However, Paul does refer to Phoebe as his *prostatis*, translated "patron." She was likely a prominent woman who assisted Paul, both socially and financially, as a necessary ally in his ministry. Since she was from a church in Corinth near a seaport, she may have assisted many who traveled through the area with lodging and other means.

In addition to Phoebe, Paul mentions eight other women in this section of greeting. "Moreover, five of these women— Prisca (v. 3), Junia (v. 7), Tryphaena and Tryphosa (v. 12), and Persis (v. 12)—are commended for their labor 'in the Lord.'"[23] This list of greetings reveals something about Paul's ministry and his relationships. He wasn't one of those theologians who would prefer to give someone a handful of money rather than spending so much of his precious time outside of his study.[24] Paul's ministry wasn't only about the sermons and the writing that he would so valuably contribute. He valued his relationships and depended on the work of many in his ministry. Among the many were women, "fellow workers in Christ Jesus" (v. 3). We see these women functioning as *ezer*s, or necessary allies, in provisional, hospitable, hardworking, nurturing, loving, and even potentially risky ways—not in a peripheral wing of the household, but alongside the men. This closing section of Paul's epistle reveals a beautiful picture of the fruit of the ministry of Word and sacrament, doesn't

---

23. Douglas J. Moo, *The Epistle to the Romans* (Grand Rapids: Eerdmans, 1996), 927.

24. This is a reference to a quote from John Cotton in Selma R. Williams, *Divine Rebel: The Life of Anne Marbury Hutchinson* (New York: Holt, Rinehart & Winston, 1981), 95.

it? And this is just a small screenshot taken from the farewell closing of one epistle. Keep this in mind as we take another snapshot—one of the targeting of women by the Christian publishing industry.

Questions for Reflection and Discussion

1. How are church officers a gift to the church?
2. Do you agree that the word *ministry* should be reserved for the particular people, means, and results of officers in the church as they serve in God's household through Word and sacrament for the maturity and unity of the faith and of the knowledge of the Son of God? If not, do you agree that this ministry should be distinguished from the other ministries in the church? If so, how would you suggest that this be done? Is there anything in the organization of the programs and initiatives in your church that you may want to reconsider in order that they might better function as the outflow of *the* ministry?
3. How can the ministerial office guide the many other important spiritual gifts of the congregants in the church?
4. What kind of authority do the officers in the church have? While there are many faithful pastors and elders in God's church, some have unfortunately been ordained who are unfit and have even abused the office. How can our ecclesiology, our theology of the church and church government, help to protect the holiness of this office and the care of the congregation?
5. *Church officers*, what do you think about using a term like *women's initiatives* instead of *women's ministries*? Do you have a plan in action to equip qualified women leaders? Are there any women in your "inner circle" of necessary allies in the ministry?

6. What are some of the ways in which women served Jesus and Paul in the ministry as necessary allies? How does that encourage you in your own service in the church? Are there other examples of women in Scripture who would embolden you in your calling as a necessary ally?

WOMEN'S MINISTRY
AS A COMMODITY

My cohosts of the Mortification of Spin podcast and I once went on a dangerous mission. We went into a Christian bookstore to broadcast live a conversation about best seller lists.[1] Okay, we only pretended to be in a Christian bookstore—but it was still pretty dangerous. Imaginary security guards were after us, and we almost didn't make it out of there with a coveted pack of Testamints™. How would we be able to share our faith *and* our passion for fresh breath with others if we couldn't get some Testamints™?

But we were really looking at a current list of Christian best sellers, and it was quite revealing. Evangelical Christians are not generally expected to be critical thinkers. And this is sad. During the show, cohost Carl Trueman observed that there's a lot of "sentimental drivel" marketed to women. As insulting

1. Carl Trueman, Todd Pruitt, and Aimee Byrd, "Bully Pulpit: Browsing the Christian Bookstore," *Mortification of Spin*, Alliance of Confessing Evangelicals, podcast audio, March 12, 2014, http://www.alliancenet.org/mos/podcast/bully-pulpit-browsing-the-christian-bookstore#.VoFyxTaYfww.

as that sounds, it is true. We did that episode a couple of years ago, but unfortunately the list of Christian best sellers looks strangely familiar, in terms of content, every time we take a gander. The best sellers list is often dominated by women authors, which in itself isn't a bad thing—but just about all the books on the list are filled with theological error. And the ones marketed especially to women appeal to the emotions and sentimentality of the reader while subverting the faithful teaching of Scripture. Does this reveal more about the women who read, about the churches that they may or may not attend, about Christian bookstores, or about Christian publishers? We all have some responsibility in this.

Women are a prime target market for Christian publishers and bookstores. In 2014, a global consumer study found that during the previous year Christian book sales grew four times as fast as those of the secular market. And women are reading more than men, buying 72 percent of Christian fiction and 59 percent of Christian nonfiction books.[2] Barna's research in 2015 continued to show that women read more than men do, revealing that almost twice as many women as men read Christian nonfiction.[3] So it makes sense to provide a good selection of Christian books for women. We have our own genre now in the Christian book market. Before the establishment of Christian trade publishers, pastors and professional theologians were the main authors of religious books. Readers would buy these books with a good idea of the confessional position and theological qualifications of the author. However, most of these books weren't written with women in mind.

2. "Onward and Upward: Christian Book Titles See Sales Rise Higher and Higher," Nielsen, August 6, 2015, http://www.nielsen.com/us/en/insights/news /2015/onward-and-upward-christian-book-titles-see-sales-rise-higher.html.

3. "The State of Books and Reading in a Digital World," Barna, October 22, 2015, https://www.barna.org/barna-update/culture/735-the-state-of-books-and -reading-in-a-digital-world#.V0RT6GOYfdk.

Interestingly, the first "trade" book that Zondervan published in 1938 was titled *The Women of the Old Testament*. The Zondervan brothers must have picked up on something while they were selling books out of the trunks of their cars.[4] Maybe there was a big consumer base of women readers. But it wasn't really until the mid-1990s that women began to break into the Christian publishing world as a popular genre of their own. By then, technology had grown enough for women like Kay Arthur, Joyce Meyer, and Beth Moore to begin to have their own ministries, radio programs, and prolific speaking engagement platforms, helping them to establish themselves enough to be able to publish.[5] These women all became best-selling authors, blazing a trail for many other women to follow.

Women like Joyce Meyer and Beth Moore, and now Lysa TerKeurst, Jen Hatmaker, Christine Caine, and Priscilla Shirer, have a charisma that is attractive to many women—and also to a significant number of men. Television, videos, and social media are used well, making them all the more engaging. They have a way of appealing to empathy, humor, and the desire to hear an entertaining story. Their friendly demeanor sends a message of trustworthiness and conveys the sense that you aren't merely buying their books and learning from their videos to get information, but are also learning from someone who is just like you or one of your friends. The combination of these gifts tends to disarm people. So they learn from them and read their books without critical discernment. And if someone does offer some criticism, it comes off as a personal attack.

4. See James E. Ruark, *The House of Zondervan: Celebrating 75 Years*, rev. ed. (Grand Rapids, Zondervan: 2006), 24–26.
5. See Karen E. Yates, "How Christian Women Are Breaking Through Traditional Book Publishing Barriers," *Washington Post*, June 8, 2015, https://www.washingtonpost.com/news/acts-of-faith/wp/2015/06/08/how-christian-women-are-breaking-through-traditional-book-publishing-barriers/.

All of a sudden, the doctrines of the church that those before us died to protect become obtuse, and the psychological jargon of our times becomes more palatable. The language of the gospel gets hijacked in order to teach personal fulfillment. That is what much of the Christian best seller list has come to, anyway. Many of the top-selling Christian books appear to have a high view of Scripture, but, once you get past the sparkling endorsements and attractive cover design, they teach extrabiblical revelation, mysticism, New Age spirituality, the prosperity gospel, or just plain bad exposition. These are not harmless books.

Women as a Stereotype

The evangelical culture has stereotyped women. So much of what is marketed as Christian literature reminds me of the airbrushed, digitally doctored, duct-taped cover models. The truth isn't good enough, so it gets a new spin. And then it sells. But is it still truth? Christians are responsible to be discerning readers, to separate the truth from the lie. Why should women be less responsible? Instead, discernment has become just as unappealing as the truth it stands up for.

It seems that we have entered an era of what I call Pinterest Christianity. We can take a Bible verse and paint it on stair risers. We can put together super-cute baptismal ceremonies with dramatic sandbag candles. We can distract people from our potentially offensive doctrines by offering our own home-made remedy and marketing it in a trendy Mason jar. We can take an Old Testament prophet and turn him into a poster boy for a great diet plan. We've become brilliant at taking the old and making it new again. We unleash the ordinary with sparkling promise that goes viral. And followers are giddy with the new revelation.

Don't get me wrong. I'm not knocking Pinterest. I happen to love it. But we shouldn't take this whimsical approach to our theology. We need to love God's truth for what it is—all of it. Because he is good.

When I was a volunteer for Care Net, I was taught a story to share about two metaphorical characters: the Truth and the Lie. One day it was so beautiful and clear outside that the Truth and the Lie decided to take a leisurely skinny-dip in the community lake. Basking in the sunshine and the tranquil air, the Truth didn't notice the Lie sneak out of the water. The Truth was so enraptured by the harmony of coexisting on a wondrous day that he was oblivious while the Lie stole his clothes from the edge of the lake. It wasn't until the Lie was completely dried off and putting on the Truth's shoes that the Truth began to see what was happening. "Hey, what are you doing? Give me back my clothes!" he yelled out.

But the Lie bolted. The Truth dashed out of the lake, chasing after the Lie, yelling all along, "Get back here and give me my clothes back!" He chased him all the way back into town, where a crowd was gathering to check out all the commotion. The Truth kept indignantly demanding his clothes back. At this point, the Lie was backed into a corner and replied, "I don't know what you are talking about; these are my clothes." The townspeople were left with a hard decision: do they believe the Lie in Truth's clothing, or do they believe the naked Truth?

Some of the latest books and movements may use Christian terminology; they may even have some important truths on display. But what is underneath all the layers of clothing? Are you willing to take a stand for the naked truth? It's usually not the easy sell.

Donald Macleod says something very important in the foreword to his book *From Glory to Golgotha*. He says, "I hope that while I still have much to learn, I don't have too much to un-learn."[6] Me too. Be careful whom you swim with!

What kind of women do we want to be known as? Another trend I have noticed in books aimed at women is the writing style itself. I'm all for throwing a sentence fragment in for effect on occasion, but some of the top-selling books marketed for women are riddled with fragments. I guess the stereotype now is that women want to read their books as if they were a Facebook feed. And they are chock-full of tweetable one-liners. To be fair, even books written for a general audience are trending this way. But remember, women are buying most of the books. Do we really want to be caricatured like this? Do we want to be known for our lack of depth? Do we want our empathetic tendencies to be pandered to, to the point where we are led by our feelings? And do we want to spend our valuable time reading a book labeled "Christian" that trivializes God's Word?

Speaking of God's Word, trivialization, and commodification, have you heard of the new Bible art journaling trend? Now, I am pro-art. There is a place for creative journaling. Some impressive note-taking and reflection make the most of this genre, even for sermon notes. I understand being inspired to paint, draw, or sculpt after spending time in God's Word. But I'm talking about turning your Bible reading into craft time.

You can buy certain Bibles that leave the outside or inside columns blank for journaling and note-taking. But now women have begun Pinterest- and Instagram-worthy doodling inside these Bibles, turning a page of Scripture into a canvas for their own muse. So, while reading the Sermon on the Mount, you may feel inspired to paint yellow and green swathes all across the page of your Bible and stencil "Consider the lilies"

---

6. Donald Macleod, *From Glory to Golgotha: Controversial Issues in the Life of Christ* (Fearn, Ross-shire, UK: Christian Focus, 2002), 7.

with your markers.[7] Maybe you would like to do a mini collage of flowers and birds on that page with magazine cutouts. These women read their Bibles with stamps, stickers, decorative masking tape, watercolors, acrylic paint, patterned scissors, decorative paper clips, glitter, and artist brush pens. The opportunities are endless! It's like scrapbooking on crack!

Doodling can be great. There are some talented doodlers out there, and that is pretty cool. Some people listen well while simultaneously doodling. But it's highly inappropriate to doodle all over God's Word. And this is doodle for show. Sure, some people like to add a visual element to learning, but this is not really a method that would help someone to truly study God's Word. So you paint an abstract scene of lilies in a field over a whole page of the Sermon on the Mount. You've then made a serious sermon, given by the Son of God himself, pretty. That hardly gets to the thrust of God's Word there—not even if you mark it with a decorative note that reads "Worry less" in calligraphy. But it's a great way to sell more specialty Bibles, along with "Christian" art supplies, and to get women excited about gathering together to show off their creative godliness. It guarantees that they will be posting shots of their "quiet time" on Pinterest and Instagram.

Something has gone terribly wrong! Why would we want to trivialize God's Word in such a way as to play dress-up with it? And what are we really learning? This creative art Bible journaling is all about me! Now most of us will never become seminary students, but do we want to remain in a perpetually elementary state of growth in the Word? It's not cute!

Women, we are made in the image of God, called to be necessary allies in his mission, not pathetic stereotypes. I may have

7. See Lauren Lanker, "Welcome to My Journaling Bible: Heart in the Margins," *The Thinking Closet* (blog), March 25, 2015, http://www.thinkingcloset.com /2015/03/25/welcome-to-my-journaling-bible-heart-in-the-margins/.

offended you in this section, but maybe we *should* be offended! This is a wake-up call. We should be growing in maturity to teach others. How are we being equipped to do this?

Biblical Womanhood and True Womanhood

In the 1980s, a considerable amount of friction developed over evangelical feminism in the church. Unfortunately, *feminist* is not a precise term anymore. People can use it to mean different things. Some use it as a compliment, and others love to sling it as the worst of insults. The word isn't particularly helpful anymore. Feminism came in several waves as a historical movement.

The first wave of feminism, in the nineteenth and early twentieth centuries, was successful in recognizing and fighting for women's rights. Finally, women were given voting rights, ownership of their children, the ability to inherit and own property and execute a will, as well as more rights in education, economics, and the workplace. I am thankful for the many Christian women and unbelievers who were involved in this movement.

Then came the 1960s. There were still some admirable gains to be made in this second wave of feminism, lasting roughly from the 1960s to the early 1980s. More attention was given to domestic abuse, leading to the passing of much-needed laws to help protect women from abuse in marriage and the workplace. Nineteenth-century ideas from the Cult of Domesticity, or True Woman movement, had still been lingering, such as these:

A really sensible woman feels her dependence. She does what she can, but she is conscious of her inferiority and therefore grateful for support.

A woman has a head almost too small for intellect but just big enough for love.

True feminine genius is ever timid, doubtful, and clingingly dependent; a perpetual childhood.[8]

These ideas were further challenged in this second wave of feminism as educational and employment opportunities expanded for women, including campaigning for equal pay. However, this wave of feminism also brought in the sexual revolution, with no-fault divorce, contraceptives, abortion rights, and gender fluidity. Also at this time, more denominations began ordaining women to the pastorate. So you can see why the church would need to speak to some of the effects of the second wave of feminism. Which parts of it were biblical and which were sinful?

And it didn't stop there. The nineties brought in a third wave of feminism that has been working to this day to enforce homosexual and transsexual ideologies, to blur God's creative design of man and woman, and to promote pornography and sexual autonomy. This wave of feminism degrades sexuality and womanhood under the banner of empowerment. So you see, feminism can mean many things, from good to deplorable.

In 1987, some evangelical leaders joined together to present a biblical response to these challenges. They formed the Council on Biblical Manhood and Womanhood (CBMW), which drafted the Danvers Statement on Biblical Manhood and Womanhood, went on to publish *Recovering Biblical Manhood and Womanhood*, and now has a website with numerous

8. Catherine J. Lavender, "Notes on The Cult of Domesticity and True Womanhood," (lecture notes, The College of Staten Island, Staten Island, NY, 1998), available online at https://csivc.csi.cuny.edu/history/files/lavender/386/truewoman.pdf.

channels, conferences, and other publications.[9] Another movement sprung up a little later, called the True Woman movement.[10] Many resources have come from these movements, through blogs, radio programs, books, conferences, and other social media.

I have been helped by some of these resources. Entering young adulthood in the early nineties, I had a lot of questions about being a Christian woman in a culture that was changing so rapidly. Many of the responses helped me when I was challenged by some of the second wave and the entire third wave of feminism. I am thankful that there is some solid academic work being offered to a popular audience that upholds the biblical equality between men and women as made in the image of God, along with maintaining the distinctions of our design. Women and men are not androgynous, and this is good. I am also thankful to have a clearer understanding of how God has set apart the office of the ministry, whereby qualified men are called to serve his church in leadership. Along with this, I am thankful for the teaching of how a husband and a wife are to reflect Christ's love to his church, with the husband representing Christ as the head of the household.

And yet, as this important conversation continues, some of these teachings are unscriptural. We may have used the teaching of biblical womanhood as a filter by which we read Scripture and look at the culture. We need to be careful not to impose teaching that is not in God's Word. Now that we have niche devotional Bibles for women, entire parachurch organizations devoted to biblical womanhood, and many books

9. See "Our History," The Council on Biblical Manhood and Womanhood, accessed December 30, 2015, http://cbmw.org/about/history/.

10. See Nancy Leigh DeMoss, *Voices of the True Woman Movement: A Call to the Counter-Revolution* (Chicago: Moody, 2010). The True Woman movement is not to be confused with the Cult of Domesticity / True Woman Movement from the 1960s, but it is curious that the same name is used.

addressing what our value and contributions are, we need to ask some questions about the movements. And I write as a woman who at first fully embraced these movements. But, as I have dug deeper into their resources and experienced some of their applications in church and evangelical parachurch culture, I see that, just like the second wave of feminism, these movements are also a mixed bag.

Is there a separate gospel for women? Everyone would answer *no* to that. But when we start getting into specific details of "gospel-driven gender roles,"[11] we may be inadvertently sending that message. Much of what is taught in the biblical womanhood movement focuses on the role of a wife and mother. While these are treasured, life-giving roles to be praised, singles and motherless wives have felt marginalized by this message, as if they cannot properly fulfill their design in biblical womanhood. Where is all the teaching on the women who left their households to follow Jesus and even provided for his ministry? Where is the teaching on Phoebe as a model of biblical womanhood, a prominent woman in society, and a patron to Paul and to many others? And, while we love the "do not be a Martha" message, much of the teaching on biblical womanhood emphasizes our domestic roles in the household. Much of my life is spent serving in domestic household roles, and I am happy that the church has worked to maintain the honor and calling of working in the home. But much less effort has been put into equipping women to be good theologians, which Jesus emphasized as the better portion.

Are there separate Bibles for women and men? Of course not. But, when we market niche devotional Bibles for men and women, we start sifting the Word of God through an unneeded filter. I am fully aware that I am reading God's

11. "Our History," Council on Biblical Manhood and Womanhood.

Word as a woman and not as a man. I even enjoy well-written and theologically helpful articles and commentary on passages with special application for women. And yet I don't want my Bible to focus on this one part of my identity. I don't want to come to God's Word only as a woman, but rather as a fellow human being made in his image. My main calling is not biblical womanhood but holiness. And having a Bible marketed specifically to me as a woman tends to send a message that it's all about me, my needs, my roles, and my womanhood.

And what the heck does *true womanhood* mean? The True Woman movement kicked off in 2008 with an assembly of over six thousand people and has expanded to regular conference events, a radio ministry, books, videos, social media, and other teaching resources. I am a woman, but am I a *true* woman? Apparently this is the question we are supposed to ask. The website that the True Woman movement has launched defines a true woman for us:

> A true woman is willing, serious, and determined to reflect the beauty and heart of Christ to her world. She seeks to live a God-centered life, trusting Him and saying "Yes, Lord!" She knows this is only possible by His grace, and seeks to do so in community, which is why we're so glad you stopped by.[12]

But how is that different from what true men should be like? Can't we say the exact same thing about Christian men? So aren't we talking about *all* Christians? Maybe what this is getting at is that a true woman recognizes both her likeness to

12. See the introduction "What Is a True Woman?" leading in to the *True Woman Blog*, Revive Our Hearts, accessed December 30, 2015, https://www.reviveour hearts.com/true-woman/.

and her distinctiveness from men, submits to the truth in righteousness regarding her design, and therefore actively participates as a necessary ally in God's mission in her church, home, and society. And there is a lot that we could write about that. But here's the other thing: when we attach "True Woman" to such a large movement and begin pumping out resources, the assumption is that all that is written is absolutely, 100 percent true. Although there are some helpful resources within this movement, in some areas much discernment is called for. I join all women who are on a quest for truth and who want to live accordingly. But movements produce celebrity, and branding can easily begin to overshadow truth. This is not a personal judgment on any particular leader, but it's something that we all need to heed—leaders and readers alike—so that we can remain discerning and seek the truth.

There will be areas in which Christians disagree in application. And this can be helpful and sharpening. You may disagree with some points in this book, but I hope that it will provoke you to further study, self-examination, and communication in your church. But do you agree with the following doctrinal statement?

> The first relationship mirrored the image of God. In the Trinity, individual and distinct beings are joined in an inseparable unity. The individual members (Father, Son, and Spirit) are joined as part of the collective whole (God).[13]

Compare that definition of the Trinity to the one in the Westminster Confession of Faith:

13. This was brought to my attention in Rachel Miller, review of *True Woman 101: Divine Design*, by Mary A. Kassian and Nancy Leigh DeMoss, *A Daughter of the Reformation* (blog), May 8, 2015, https://adaughterofthereformation.wordpress.com/2015/05/08/true-woman-101-divine-design/.

In the unity of the Godhead there be three Persons of one substance, power, and eternity: God the Father, God the Son, and God the Holy Ghost.[14]

Do you see the serious error? The Father, the Son, and the Holy Spirit are not three separate beings! The church has preserved the orthodox teaching that the Westminster Confession affirms in its definition of the Trinity. This is an important truth about who God is, one that we should not be sloppy with or take lightly. If the authors were men, do you think there would be more critical engagement with a book like this? If we are going to have a movement based on true womanhood, the first thing we need to examine is the content of the teaching. And this is an area in which the authors, the publishers, the parachurch organizations, the Christian bookstores, the readers, and the churches that use the books for teaching material need to take responsibility. Teachers, readers, publishers, and merchants can have good intentions and still be in error.

Pastors and Elders, What Kind of Women Do You Want in Your Church?

Pastors and elders want thinking women in the church, right? And yet popular beliefs that came out of the nineteenth century's cult of domesticity still seem to linger in the evangelical culture today. Back then, people taught that women's brains were inferior to men's intellectually and that women needed to reserve their energy and blood flow for reproductive purposes.[15] These are ideas we usually joke about now,

14. WCF 2.3.
15. See Lavender, "Notes on the Cult of Domesticity."

even to provoke a woman in innocent fun, because we know them to be scientifically proven false. And yet, even as the Reformed church is known for its more robust, theological teaching, there still seems to be some residue from the nineteenth-century worldview of a woman's physical, intellectual, and emotional capabilities. While we pay lip service to the importance of competent women in the church, there doesn't seem to be much outrage over the quality of their resources. How can the officers of the church engage with the market of theological material for women? Here are a few suggestions to begin with.

Realize That Women Are Thirsty to Learn—the Market Has!

More women than men are buying Christian books. Over six thousand women gathered for the first True Woman conference. The Gospel Coalition has also joined in to host biannual women's conferences with big numbers. Also capitalizing on this momentum, another "movement" has sprung up, with the promise to disciple women of the new generation, called the IF: Gathering.[16] Best-selling women's author Jennie Allen "sensed God telling her to disciple a generation,"[17] which led to other best-selling authors Ann Voskamp and Jen Hatmaker joining her in the establishment of the IF: Gathering. There are also the popular Women of Faith conferences that began back in 1986 and are well marketed and attended by thousands of women. They also have conferences for teens now. While this book has raised concerns about the commodification of

16. See Aimee Byrd, "A New Tribe?" *Housewife Theologian* (blog), Alliance of Confessing Evangelicals, June 21, 2013, http://www.alliancenet.org/mos/housewife -theologian/a-new-tribe#.VobJQzaYfww.

17. "Who We Are," IF: Gathering, accessed January 1, 2016, https://ifgathering .com/who-we-are/.

women in publishing, movements, and coalitions, the impressive size of their events and resources points to the fact that women are eager to learn more as Christ's disciples. That is really great news.

Church officers should be paying attention to this, because the primary place where discipleship should be taking place is in the local church. Along with the conferences and events, there is another trend that has grown in women's ministries, exemplified by Community Bible Studies (CBS) and Bible Study Fellowship (BSF). These are interdenominational, global organizations that focus on equipping Christians in Bible study. CBS is strictly for women, while BSF started as a women's Bible study but is no longer restricted to women. Many women who desire to be more disciplined and to go deeper in their Bible study have joined a local CBS or BSF group. While these are international organizations, local churches generally host their regular meetings. There are many benefits that can come from being a part of these organizations. The lessons are Word-centered, and they aim to equip leaders with Bible study skills to serve in their local churches. Since these organizations have the more narrow focus of studying the Bible in a local context, there isn't as much of a problem with celebrity personalities and branding, which can easily overshadow and corrupt parachurch operations. The local leaders are volunteers, so there isn't a financial factor that can cloud their judgment.

Without discouraging women from being a part of these groups, I do want to ask some questions about how we can utilize the resources of and involvement in an interdenominational community study, parachurch ministries, and Christian publishing, while keeping the local church and its doctrinal distinctives as a priority in discipleship. Women are thirsty to learn and be discipled—so much so that we have looked outside of our local churches for help. That's not a horrible thing—churches cannot do it all! Church officers need resources too, and parachurch organizations can help to provide them.

With the mission of the local church in mind, we can look at these resources in their own context. The church is commissioned to make disciples through the ministry of Word and sacrament. You don't want to outsource your discipling privileges and responsibilities to parachurch organizations, but you do want to encourage and incorporate the use of helpful resources and opportunities to further teach the women in your church. Capitalize on this wonderful desire that women have to learn, but help to equip them to be discerning, even within the evangelical culture around us. Parachurch organizations are supposed to serve the church and, in many cases, the outside community. It's imperative that we keep the right perspective there, because they do it without the oversight of the officers of the church.

Women Need to Have the Same Theological Standards as Men.

It may sound like a no-brainer that men and women should have the same theological standards. But in my writing and speaking experiences, I get a sense of the theological climate in confessional churches, and it's disappointing. I get to meet many wonderful women in churches just like yours. A lot of them sit under good preaching. I've made numerous friends through these opportunities. And I will tell you that the women who take good theology seriously are discouraged by what is offered for women's studies in their churches. Some have suffered through books with blatantly bad theology, and others are just longing for something with more depth. Some of the leaders have expressed a desire for better training to teach. We want to be well equipped and counted on as necessary allies, not dismissed as nonintellectuals who are satisfied with fluff. When a top-selling and well-endorsed book aimed at discipling women teaches that the Trinity consists of three beings, many of us are insulted by the lack of care and oversight given to the production of our resources.

I don't think that this has happened because pastors don't care what their women are reading. Although feminism came in three waves over the course of a century, that third wave hit us pretty ferociously, and it really affected the church. All of a sudden, pastors have been under a lot more pressure to answer questions about women in the ministry, sexuality, gender distinction, and, yes, women's roles and men's roles. At the same time, the Christian publishing and parachurch organizations started turning out many resources to help. Most of the resources dealing with doctrine that are attractive to the women in our churches promote Christian values that we hold dear. But in many cases, the cart has been put before the horse—the imperatives have gone before the indicatives that carry them. Books that teach Christian living emphasize ideals that we would wholeheartedly want to see taught in the church: purity, faithfulness to our spouses, investing in our children and raising them up in the ways of the Lord, and the ordination of qualified men to the ministry. Some books write on these topics well. Others, especially books for women's ministry, reduce Christian theology to domestic roles, the social gospel, the vigor of our affections, mysticism, and more. Who knew that there were so many ways to be reductionistic? Yet there seems to be a lack of substantial studies written for women or by women on important topics such as the attributes of God, the doctrine of Scripture, the person and work of Jesus Christ, the Trinity, the doctrines of grace, church history, or eschatology. That leads to the next point.

We Need to Read More Than Women's Resources.

There are many wonderful books written on these topics, and we don't need to grab all of our resources from the women's ministry genre. We are really missing out if we don't check out a broader range of reading. Throughout the church's history, pastor-theologians have written most of the best books on these topics. They have had the education, the time devoted to the ministry of the Word, and the pastoral experience to help the church on these subjects.

Church officers, encourage your women to be well read and well rounded. If you have read a book that has impacted your theology and spiritual growth, why not lead a small group or book discussion on it? You may or may not want to share this book exclusively with the women's group. There are simple ways to promote an intentional, active reading culture in your church. Show the women in your congregation that you care what they are reading by simply inquiring about it in casual conversation. As you learn about their interests and struggles, you will have opportunities to suggest helpful books to them. Such conversations will impress upon them that their church officers value and wish to promote their theological growth. It's encouraging to hear pastors recommending books for their congregants to read. What a great way to encourage the whole congregation! Why not share some book reviews, both positive and critical, on the church website or church group's Facebook page, or in the church newsletter or weekly emails? You could take it one step further by asking congregants to submit reviews of the books they are reading, with the possibility of sharing them with the congregation as well. This will encourage congregants to read with discernment and could become a great help to you as a pastor. After all, you can't read everything that's out there; but, if you have a handful of people in your church, both women and men, who are gifted at reviewing books, you will get a wider sampling of the market.

While women need to read more than women's resources, keep in mind that there are some wonderful books and Bible studies written by women.[18] Check the footnote provided below, where I have shared some of those resources for *Ordained Servant Online*. I recommend that pastors and elders read some of these titles; you may even learn a thing or two. But that is a topic for the next chapter.

Questions for Reflection and Discussion

1. What responsibilities would you say that each of these groups has when it comes to the Christian book market: women (consumers), their churches, Christian bookstores, Christian publishers, parachurch ministries? And which of them can you do something about?

2. Why do you think that women are buying more Christian books than men are?

3. When you buy a Christian book written by a woman, is her denominational affiliation important to you? What guidelines do you use to evaluate whether the author may be making a good contribution, or whether she is in error or full of fluff?

4. Was there ever a time in your discipleship when you realized you had some bad theology that you needed to unlearn? What made you realize this, and what steps did you take to separate the truth from the error?

5. What kind of woman do you want to be known as? Does a

---

18. I have shared some titles here: Aimee Byrd, "Nurturing Theologically Rich Women's Initiatives in Your Church," *Ordained Servant Online*, The Orthodox Presbyterian Church. December 2015, http://www.opc.org/os.html?article_id=520&issue_id=110.

fun-loving or artsy person need to lack theological depth? How would the opposite be true?

6. Did I say anything in this chapter that got under your skin? Are there some areas in which you disagree with me? Enter the conversation by explaining your argument.

7. How have parachurch organizations been helpful to you? Are there any ways in which they could serve the church better?

8. *Church officers*, I have been hitting some of the same points about the Christian market hard throughout this book—particularly your responsibility to engage with it for the sake of the women in your church. But I understand that it can be overwhelming. My passion to encourage women to be responsible theologians has led me to get into this very industry, trying to provide good resources. Thank you for taking the time to read this book and for your work in shepherding the women in your church. What do you see as the biggest challenges and the most helpful resources as you think more critically about this topic and how it relates specifically to your congregation?

PART THREE

Working toward a Solution

MEN LEARNING
FROM WOMEN?

"Do you believe it is okay for a woman to think and write about theology, given she will also be read by men such as myself? If so, why is it not allowed for a woman to preach?" This was a question that a man asked in the comments section of one of my *Housewife Theologian* blog posts. I've been asked similar questions before. If women are not to preach, are they permitted to teach in an environment where men will be learning?

Let's begin with the first part of the question, which I'm hoping we would all easily agree on. Every person is a theologian, whether that person is a man or a woman. To use a double negative, I can't not think about theology. Theology is the study of God—knowing God. If Jesus really prayed, "And this is eternal life, that they *know* you, the only true God, and Jesus Christ whom you have sent" (John 17:3), then every one of us had better be serious about being a good theologian. My eternal life doesn't depend on my pastor's relationship with God, my father's relationship with God, or my husband's relationship with God. I am responsible to know God, to repent of my sins, to recognize his grace, to depend on Christ alone for holiness, and to trust in his Spirit as I live a life of faith and obedience. My eternal life depends on my own relationship with God. Everyone is a theologian, and we should be good ones who know God rightly according to his Word.

I'm not sure what my commenter's view is regarding women's ordination. There are many roles for women in the church, but Scripture makes it clear that the offices of elder and pastor are not among them (see 1 Tim. 2:12). Women are not the only ones excluded by God's Word from the office of ministry; most men are never called to this position, either (see 1 Tim. 3:1–7). God has ordained this for our good. With that said, if we are serious about the distinctiveness of men and women, and if we really do believe that women are created to be necessary allies, then above all we should want to equip competent, theologically minded, thinking women, which has been the theme of this whole book.

Is there a difference between preaching God's Word and reflecting on it, explaining it, writing about it, and even teaching it in a different setting? Yes! If it is done faithfully, we are talking about a difference between the authority of the Word of God and the authority of the word of man. Could a woman compose and deliver a sermon-worthy exposition of Scripture that would enlighten those listening? Sure, many women could! But this is not our calling. And besides, delivering a good exposition of Scripture is not the only responsibility of being a preacher. Paul explained to the elders of the Ephesian church that they were shepherds, not just sermon deliverers (see Acts 20:28). But when they do preach, it comes with the authority of the Word of God to his people. I do not lead authoritatively from a pulpit. The office of pastor is different from any other teaching. Pastors are set apart by a special calling to proclaim God's Word (1 Thess. 2:13) in a context in which God promises to bless us in Christ.

So, as for women not having authority to teach a man, this has to do with the authority of the ordained ministerial office. Outside of this, we are foolish to think that men do not learn from women. How can we be allies if we are not all teachers of some sort? And considering all the influence that women have in the church, the home, and the world, we should want them to be very good theologians.

I am the product of God's Word being received. I take that closing benediction seriously, and I am so enthralled by what I have received that I can't keep quiet during the week. I must reflect on it. I must learn more about this amazing God. And I want to share that with others. God gifts many people to be teachers. And he gifts many of those to write. But praise God for the ministerial office of preaching and ruling elders! Let's leave that to those whom he calls.

When Men Are Instructed by a Woman

I'm going to take things one step further by saying that men *ought* to learn from women. There has been some troubling teaching under the banner of biblical womanhood that concerns me. Nowhere in Scripture do we read that all women should submit to all men. So why would we teach that "at the heart of mature femininity is a freeing disposition to affirm, receive and nurture strength and leadership from worthy men in ways appropriate to a woman's differing relationships"?[1] I am not constantly looking for male leadership in my life. I am a married woman and a member of a church, and I understand

1. John Piper, "A Vision of Biblical Complementarity," in *Recovering Biblical Manhood and Womanhood: A Response to Evangelical Feminism*, ed. John Piper and Wayne Grudem (1991; repr., Wheaton, IL: Crossway, 2006), 46.

the order needed in a household, but male leadership does not define my femininity. I'm not looking to my male neighbors, coworkers, or mail carriers to nurture their leadership. This kind of teaching perpetuates a constant authority/submission dynamic between men and women that can be very harmful. And because of it, there have been even stranger applications, such as why it would be okay for a man to ask directions from a housewife in her backyard if he were lost.[2] Why would this even be a question? Because of the teaching that "to the degree that a woman's influence over man is personal and directive it will generally offend a man's good, God-given sense of responsibility and leadership, and thus controvert God's created order."[3] We must ask, where is this taught in God's Word?

Certainly Scripture does not have women leading in the ministerial office in worship, but we do see plenty of women giving personal and directive guidance to men outside of the service. And we even have men being rebuked for not listening. When Jesus first appeared to Mary Magdalene after his resurrection, he instructed her to go to his disciples with the good news (see John 20:17). Jesus could have appeared to his disciples first, but he didn't. He appeared to Mary and told her to instruct the men with specific information. But, in their grief, the men would not believe what she told them (see Mark 16:11). When he did appear to the disciples, Jesus rebuked them for not believing those who had told them about his resurrection (see Mark 16:14; see also Luke 24). Is it okay for men to learn from women? "God, of course, may have His own opinion, but the Church is reluctant to endorse it."[4]

Even in marriage, we have the beautiful example of Priscilla

---

2. See ibid., 50.

3. Ibid., 51.

4. Dorothy Sayers, *Are Women Human?* (1971; repr., Grand Rapids: Eerdmans, 2005), 67.

and Aquila. Actually, this couple gives us a glimpse of Christian marriage, the church, and secular vocations. We are introduced to them in Acts 18, where we learn that they are tentmakers who have moved to Corinth from Italy. From then on, it is interesting to note that this married couple is mentioned with Priscilla's name first, every time but once.[5] We wouldn't expect that. There have been speculations that she was the prominent one socially, or maybe in their tent-making business. No one knows for sure, but Luke and Paul both wrote it that way. Paul stayed with this couple while he was in Corinth, since all three of them were tentmakers. Here we have a great picture of husband and wife, working together in this trade. Priscilla wasn't just fetching the coffee while listening to the men's wise words and admiring their providing skills; she was a fellow worker. She had a job as a tentmaker. That doesn't sound very feminine, according to some of the teaching for married Christian women today.

Paul calls them "fellow workers in Christ Jesus, who risked their necks for my life, to whom not only I give thanks but all the churches of the Gentiles give thanks as well" (Rom. 16:3–4). He then mentions the church that meets in the home of Priscilla and Aquila. So this married couple got their hands dirty making tents and in missionary work with Paul. They made an impact on the Gentiles, and they eventually opened their home for the church to worship in. That's pretty impressive. And Priscilla was a fellow worker in it all. She was no little woman.

We also learn that Priscilla was a fellow theologian. The couple traveled with Paul to Ephesus, and when the dynamic, Alexandrian Apollos spoke, Priscilla and Aquila noticed that something wasn't quite right. They were discerning. They recognized that Apollos was competent to teach what he knew, the baptism of John, but they also realized that he was missing

5. See Acts 18:18, 26; Rom. 16:3; 1 Cor. 16:19; 2 Tim. 4:19.

the rest of the story. Seeing that this man was a godly, good teacher, they pulled him aside and taught him "the way of God more accurately" (Acts 18:26). We don't read that Aquila took Apollos aside man-to-man for this instruction and correction. No, we see that Priscilla and Aquila approached Apollos together (her name first), resulting in much fruit. Apollos became a great preacher who watered the seed that Paul planted (see 1 Cor. 3:6). But first, he humbled himself to learn from a couple of tentmakers, one being a woman. Priscilla did not have an attitude to subvert his role as a preacher and take his position. But she played a major role as a necessary ally to help this preacher. And he listened to her. Calvin goes so far as to say, "One of the chief teachers of the Church was instructed by a woman."[6]

A Song and a Prayer

There are two women in Scripture who have taught us all rich theology through a song and a prayer. Mary's Magnificat and Hannah's prayer reveal just how competent these women were in God's Word. They begin with praise and thanksgiving and then burst into glorious confession. And these two prayers are very similar. We see in Hannah's prayer a foreshadowing of what is to come. While she is certainly praying in the context of her own life, and while the significance of the prayer is evident in 1 and 2 Samuel, the themes of this prayer are further played out in Mary's song, as they point to the birth of the Savior of both women.

Hannah desperately wanted a child, but "the Lord had closed her womb" (1 Sam. 1:5). Her husband, Elkanah, had another wife who mocked Hannah for her inability to have children. In

6. John Calvin, *Commentary upon the Acts of the Apostles*, vol. 2, in *Acts 14–28, Romans 1–16*, trans. Henry Beveridge, Calvin's Commentaries 19 (repr., Grand Rapids: Baker, 2003), 202.

her extreme sadness, Hannah prayed to the Lord, vowing that if he would bless her with a son, she would devote him to the Lord. She prayed with such passion that the priest thought she was drunk. Scripture tells us that when she returned home and "Elkanah knew Hannah his wife . . . the LORD remembered her" (1 Sam. 1:19). When it became time for Hannah to "lend" her son to the Lord, she prayed again. You would expect this prayer to be all about the miraculous opening of her womb, the blessings of motherhood, the beauty and wonder of Samuel her son, and the anxieties of now giving him back to the Lord. But that's not what she prays. She opens with praises to the Lord and then speaks of his person and work. It is all about the Lord!

After Mary and Elizabeth rejoice together over the miracle of Mary's virginal pregnancy and her carrying of the Savior, she does the same. Mary's song is strikingly similar to Hannah's. Just look at some of the similarities:

> *Hannah*: "My heart exults in the LORD . . . I rejoice in your salvation" (1 Sam. 2:1).
> *Mary*: "My soul magnifies the Lord, and my spirit rejoices in God my Savior" (Luke 1:46–47).

> *Hannah*: "My horn is exalted in the LORD" (1 Sam. 2:1).
> *Mary*: ". . . for he who is mighty has done great things for me" (Luke 1:49a).

> *Hannah*: "There is none holy like the LORD" (1 Sam. 2:2).
> *Mary*: ". . . and holy is his name" (Luke 1:49b).

> *Hannah*: "The LORD makes poor and makes rich; he brings low and he exalts. He raises up the poor from the dust; he lifts the needy from the ash heap to make them sit with princes and inherit a seat of honor" (1 Sam. 2:7–8).

Mary: "He has brought down the mighty from their thrones and exalted those of humble estate" (Luke 1:52).

Hannah: "Those who were full have hired themselves out for bread, but those who were hungry have ceased to hunger" (1 Sam. 2:5).
Mary: "He has filled the hungry with good things, and the rich he has sent away empty" (Luke 1:53).

This is certainly no coincidence! Mary adopted some of Hannah's expressions, as they were worshipping the same God. The same God who remembered insignificant Hannah in her barrenness favored the young virgin Mary to conceive and bear "the Son of the Most High" (Luke 1:32). While the two women were in different circumstances eleven hundred years apart, we have here two significant pregnancies being celebrated by two formerly insignificant women, and two sons who were dedicated to the work of God. Both these songs teach us about praise, the holiness of God, his wondrous mercy, our salvation in the Lord, his great faithfulness to his people, and the sovereignty and power of God in his will and judgments. It is a blessing to have the examples of women like Mary Magdalene, Phoebe, Lydia, Martha, Mary, the woman at the well, Junia, and Priscilla to point to as some practical examples of necessary allies in the church. Hannah and Mary provide us with theological treatises, dressed up as songs of praise and prayer, that are recorded in Scripture for both men and women to learn from.

Women and Sketchy Theology

Sadly, most of the teaching coming from our current top-selling women's books and speakers is way off the mark from Mary and Hannah. There are many women, just like there are many men, whom we should not learn from. I have been reading a lot of these popular books in the Christian genre, and I have also been reading up on some of the more notorious women in American church history, such as Anne Hutchinson and Aimee Semple McPherson. There is a common thread in the bad theology: these women have all claimed to have received special revelation from God.

Let's start with Anne Hutchinson. There is much about this woman to admire—particularly her desire to take theology seriously and to demonstrate how what we believe to be true about the person and work of Jesus Christ shapes our everyday living. Anne challenged the patriarchy in her day while also striving to live as a godly woman, wife, and mother. She was passionate to continue a discussion after a church sermon had ended, examining Scripture and even longing to engage more with the pastor about the doctrines he taught. She resisted the legalism, bad theology, and politics in England, to the point where, at forty-three years of age, she traveled with her family from England to the New World. Anne Hutchinson's story is complicated and nuanced.[7] The New World apparently wasn't ready for a woman like her. In 1638, she was excommunicated from the Puritan church and banished from the Massachusetts Bay Colony, "denounced as a liar, a leper, and the Devil's helper."[8]

One of Anne's tactics to be heard was to claim direct revelations from God. It was difficult for a woman's views and contributions to be taken seriously, and this was a way to get even the men to listen. At first she appealed mainly to women, who would gather at her home to discuss John Cotton's sermons. After all, she got the impression that

7. I encourage you to read a biography, such as Selma R. Williams, *Divine Rebel: The Life of Anne Marbury Hutchinson* (New York: Holt, Rinehart & Winston, 1981).
8. Ibid., 185.

Cotton preferred being isolated in his study to being bothered with such personal interactions. And "'the godly mag-
istrates and the elders of the church . . . winked at . . . her
practice' for several months, even though her audiences grew
larger and larger till she was seen as accommodating in her
cramped living room almost every woman in Boston, and
some from neighboring towns too."[9] Why would the church
officers wink at women who wanted to have more depth in
their learning? Many of these women were attracted to Anne
because they were "frustrated by the intellectual stagnation
that was their lot as outsider."[10] Here we have the women
kept at arm's length from the ministry, left without oversight
in a peripheral existence where it was no big deal what they
were learning. But Anne's message, accompanied by her special revelations from God, soon began reaching the men as
well. In just two years, she had "the strongest constituency of
any leader in the whole colony."[11]

But let's fast-forward a couple hundred years to a woman
from Canada who attracted exponentially larger crowds of
men and women with far less substance to her theology:

In 1926, "her people" numbered in the scores of thousands, and millions more regularly followed her activities via radio, newsreels, and the press. Whatever she did
seemed newsworthy. On average, she made the front
page of America's biggest newspapers three times a week
throughout the 1920s. . . . Mayors welcomed her; judges,
lawyers, and professors endorsed and introduced her;
churches of all Protestant denominations sponsored her
evangelistic efforts. Opposition only fanned curiosity. By

9. Ibid., 96.
10. Ibid.
11. Ibid., 121.

1919, the largest auditoriums in the country could not hold the crowds that thronged her meetings.[12]

Who was she? She was Aimee Semple McPherson, the Pentecostal celebrity evangelist who established the International Church of the Foursquare Gospel. Many women can still identify with Aimee's conflicting desires—wanting to be that ideal woman, much of which would culminate in the roles of wife and mother, while also consumed by ambitions that took her outside the home. So she found an authoritative voice that silenced anyone who would disagree with her choices: she claimed that God had revealed to her that she was to "go" serve him with her gifts of preaching, evangelization, and the speaking and interpretation of tongues. Aimee claimed direct revelations from God as the authority behind much of her teaching and decision making. But when you compare what she taught to God's Word in Scripture, there are all kinds of discrepancies.

That is what we see in much of contemporary Christian women's best sellers. And many of these women are appealing to the Reformed community. Sarah Young's devotional book, *Jesus Calling*, which has sold well over ten million copies, explains that she wanted more communication from God than just the Bible. She wanted to "receive messages during [her] times of communing with God."[13] This devotional book records these messages and pairs them with Scripture. Young holds a master's degree from the PCA's Covenant Seminary, which would make one think she would not teach that God gives direct revelation outside Scripture in this age of the church. Maybe that's why so many in the Reformed

12. Edith L. Blumhofer, *Aimee Semple McPherson: Everybody's Sister* (Grand Rapids: Eerdmans, 1993), 3.
13. Sarah Young, *Jesus Calling* (Nashville: Thomas Nelson, 2004), xi–xii.

denominations have not looked into her teaching. Beth Moore has been a go-to for many women's Bible studies through her Living Proof Ministries. This is an organization that partners with LifeWay Christian Resources, a branch of the Southern Baptist Convention and one of the largest producers of Christian resources. Moore constantly uses her conversations with God, with his personal words to her in quotations, as a basis for her teaching. Priscilla Shirer, the daughter of popular pastor Tony Evans, also teaches as someone who has heard God's "whisperings,"[14] connecting the authority of her own teaching to obedience to God's revelation for her to teach "many people . . . refreshed, renewed focus and fervency of prayer they'd never known before."[15]

Shirer's book *Fervent* contrasts sharply with the prayer of Hannah. Young's book of devotions, recording her times enjoying God's presence, contrasts sharply with Mary's song of praise as the Son of God was still present in her womb. Hannah's and Mary's theological contributions focus on the character of God, confessing the timeless truths that apply to all God's people. Shirer, Young, and company focus more on a personal word that is customized for them and on how they deliver their prayers and live their Christian lives fervently, audaciously, or unglued.[16] If these women were hearing direct revelations from God, you'd expect some better theology. But that is not the case.

You may be wondering why I would be making such a strong case about women and bad theology in a chapter encouraging men to learn from them. Well, I have some

14. See Priscilla Shirer, *Fervent: A Woman's Battle Plan for Serious, Specific, and Strategic Prayer* (Nashville: B&H, 2015), 188.

15. Ibid., 186.

16. See Shirer, *Fervent*; Beth Moore, *Audacious* (Nashville: B&H, 2015); Lysa TerKeurst, *Unglued: Making Wise Choices in the Midst of Raw Emotions* (Grand Rapids: Zondervan, 2012).

layered points to make. First of all, we do need to be paying attention to everyone we are learning from. We are responsible for our own maturity in the Word and for discernment in reading and listening (see Acts 17:11). It's not okay for anyone to learn bad theology, no matter what our gender or the gender of our teacher may be. No one should be winking at any of this. We shouldn't accept bad theology just for the sake of encouraging women to teach. All teachers should have the same standards for content and methods.

Do we take women seriously? Everyone reading this book is nodding his or her head right now, of course. That's why you picked up this book in the first place. But this is a question worth examining with more insight than our first reactions may give. The women mentioned above are teachers who add an authority to their words and decisions based on alleged personal revelation from God. They may do this because they know that they wouldn't be taken seriously otherwise. When they add the weight of God's personal revelation to their words, all of a sudden more people are listening. Do we really have to do that in order to attract attention to what we have to say? Will people interact with insights and opinions that are merely our own?

And, when we do interact, can we do it on the basis of what is said, not the personality or gender of who is saying it? If we take women seriously, we will want them to be good teachers of the Word. So often, the theology of women such as these is not critiqued because we don't want to hurt feelings. Somehow it comes off as not nice to critique a woman's teaching. Well, that isn't taking women seriously, either. It is not insulting to point out error. What is unloving is giving a teacher license to teach falsely because you like her personality, because you want to believe that it's true, or, worse, because you don't want to engage critically with a woman.

Teachers will be accountable before God for what they say, so we should want to correct them.

Scripture assures us that we do not need to look for any extra revelations from God. We already have a special word from God in the Bible. And since the canon of God's Word is now complete and available to us, there is no new thing that we need to hear.

> All Scripture is breathed out by God and profitable for teaching, for reproof, for correction, and for training in righteousness, that the man of God may be complete, equipped for every good work. (2 Tim. 3:16–17)

We don't need to ask for a personal voice from God. He would have us do the hard work of learning his Word and becoming so familiar with it, through time and study in it, that we know him and his character well. He would have us regularly assemble to hear his Word authoritatively preached to us in the context of the covenant community of our local church. He would have us serve one another in this context and under the oversight of the ministry. Through this process, and with the Spirit's enabling, we grow in wisdom as we apply these truths in our everyday experiences. This will then inform our teaching and decision making. We don't wait for a feeling or for audible whispers; we can *go* to God's Word! And that is how we are to test the teaching of others.[17]

So none of us gets a "God told me" pass. We don't gain authority by claiming a special revelation from God. God's word in Scripture is our authority. Let's listen to what women

17. For a helpful introduction to the sufficiency of Scripture, see Kevin DeYoung, *Taking God at His Word* (Wheaton, IL: Crossway Books, 2014). For a more academic study of the doctrine of Scripture, see Peter A. Lillback and Richard B. Gaffin Jr., eds., *Thy Word Is Still Truth* (Phillipsburg, NJ: P&R, 2013).

have to share according to God's revealed word in Scripture, and let's take that seriously.

Authority, Submission, and Parachurch Conferences

There's also some doctrinal teaching under the banner of authority and submission that concerns me. We've already looked at the theme of headship and household in Scripture, as well as at Paul's teaching in Ephesians 5 that the marriage relationship is a picture of Christ's love for his church. But we need to be careful not to reduce a woman's entire role in life to what a wife pictures. Primarily, we are told from the creation account that women are made in the image of God, and this is very important. Some teachers want to use the model of the Trinity to teach the submission of all women to all men. This is an area in which we need to be careful, because, when we are talking about Christ's voluntary submission to the Father in the plan of salvation, we are speaking of what theologians call the *economic Trinity*. This refers to the roles that the three persons have agreed to fulfill in the economy (management) of our salvation. But when we talk about the *ontological Trinity*, or who God is in his being, there isn't any Scripture telling us that the Son plays a submissive role.[18]

This is important to understand when we are talking about who God is, and it is important in making applications to men and women. The Bible teaches an economy in household management: there needs to be a head who is responsible to carry out its mission as the other members actively participate within

18. For a good introduction to where this is being taught, see Rachel Miller, review of *True Woman 101: Divine Design*, by Mary A. Kassian and Nancy Leigh DeMoss, *A Daughter of the Reformation* (blog), May 8, 2015, https://adaughterofthe reformation.wordpress.com/2015/05/08/true-woman-101-divine-design/.

their roles. But it does not teach an ontological authority of all men over all women. Wendy Alsup is helpful in explaining how important it is to distinguish between the metaphor that marriage gives us and the essence of who we really are:

> Our essence, male and female, is that we were both created in the image of God. Our essence, also, is that both male and female are in reality the Church. Neither of us are in essence Jesus; we are both in essence the Church. And both of us were created to image God. We can not zoom in on Ephesians 5 and treat it as the whole on gender. We can not treat it as the context for all other discussion on gender. God sets the context in Genesis 1–2, a context in which Paul writes the whole of Ephesians.[19]

This is important as we consider relationships between men and women in our everyday lives, as well as the topic of men learning from women. Women can have vocations in which they are men's bosses, and that is not discordant with Scripture. Women can write books and articles that men can learn from. They can teach a class and have male students. And if a postman comes to my door, his only authority over me relates to his position in the United States Postal Service; it has nothing to do with his being a man. If a postwoman tells my husband that he did not use proper postage to deliver a package, she would not be insulting his manhood. He would need to submit to her direct and personal guidance.[20]

---

19. Wendy Alsup, review of *True Woman 101: Divine Design*, by Mary A. Kassian and Nancy Leigh DeMoss, *Practical Theology for Women* (blog), March 14, 2015, http://www.theologyforwomen.org/2015/03/my-review-of-true-woman-101.html.

20. See Aimee Byrd, "John Piper's Advice For Women in the Workforce," *Housewife Theologian* (blog), Alliance of Confessing Evangelicals, August 17, 2015, http://www.alliancenet.org/mos/housewife-theologian/john-pipers-advice-for-women-in-the-workforce#.VpAIwTaYfww.

But since Scripture does highlight that women are not to be ordained in the authoritative office of ministry, one to which all women and men are to submit, things get a little confusing when it comes to parachurch events. Most of the conferences hosted by parachurch organizations that hold to the scriptural teaching of male eldership in the church do not invite women speakers to coed events. Women may be invited to speak in a workshop breakout, usually on a topic related to women's issues, but not to talk about general theology at the main sessions. One way that parachurch organizations have sought to give women more speaking opportunities is to host women's conferences. This is also a way to avoid having men sitting under their teaching, as men are not allowed to attend.

But this setup invokes a lot of questions. Is a parachurch conference equivalent to a worship service? Should we be setting them up that way? Some do have that feel. There may be more formal dress, opening prayer, the singing of hymns and spiritual songs, and then—sermons? Well, many of the speakers are preachers. If the conference is to be like a worship service, then we are going to want someone who is ordained delivering the "sermon." But in parachurch conferences, there are usually multiple speakers. It's easy to see how the lineup would consist of all men in this format.

Let's take a look at the format of parachurch conferences functioning as worship services. First, let's think about whether there is any good in it. There are many Christians whom I love but do not get the chance to worship with. In an idealistic way, a parachurch conference set up as a worship service gives me a picture of heaven. We may not have the lion lying down with the lamb, but we do have the Presbyterians worshipping with the Baptists. That's huge! We get to hear preachers whom we wouldn't normally hear. We get to have church on Friday night. And, after all, it is worshipful to sing to the Lord together, to pray together, and to hear teaching from his Word.

And yet there are some good reasons to distinguish between parachurch conferences and worship services. Now, I'm someone who wants to have her cake and eat it too. (I mean, if I get to have cake, it's basically torture not to let me eat it. But for some reason that is the well-known expression that we would use for a situation like this.) Parachurch organizations are not churches. There is no office of elders in a parachurch organization—only board members. Interestingly, in my experience, these board members are all male. There is no one pastor who is faithfully preaching expositional sermons over long periods of time. There are guest speakers, often all speaking on a related topic within a few days and then flying home. And while some elements of the worship liturgy can be used in a parachurch conference, other critical elements are left out. We do not have the congregational prayer of the local church. There usually isn't a time for confession and assurance of pardon, there may or may not be a call to worship, the sacraments of baptism and the Lord's Supper are not administered, and there is no benediction. So these parachurch organizations do not have all the elements of a worship service, even when they mimic one.

And this is where it gets more interesting. The main reason for not having women speakers is that these organizations do not want to give the appearance of a woman teaching with authority over a man. However, there doesn't seem to be a problem with giving the appearance of a worship service without providing all the elements in worship, which is the context in which God promises to bless us in Christ. A board of directors does not have the responsibility or the authority to shepherd conference attendees. So what kind of authority are we talking about here? Granted, some of these organizations would have a problem with women teaching men even if their conferences weren't confused with the worship service. But those who rightly want to protect the authority of the ministerial offices of the church, but who do not go beyond the biblical parameters of headship and household, may be undermining the very offices they are trying to protect. Hannah Anderson asked this question about authority in parachurch organizations, making some good points:

> Applications about teaching and authority only make sense in context of a community **that actually possesses authority**. Some would say to simply "err on the safe side" and apply the dynamics of local church ministry to parachurch organizations. But doing this may actually minimize the significance of the local church the same way that calling a woman to submit to all men diminishes the significance of her submission to her own husband.[21]

Because we want to protect these household structures and don't want to host anything that would cause such confusion, we should clarify what the parachurch function is. An "err on the safe side" argument doesn't make any sense. Why should we be content with erring on *any* side? If we go to a parachurch conference, it is not the same as if we were just visiting a different congregation for the evening. We should be upfront about the differences and work at giving the appearance of what we are actually doing.

The same error can be made in the opposite direction at women's retreats. When I'm invited to speak at a retreat, it's

---

21. Hannah Anderson, "Complementarian Organizations and Where Women Belong," *The Gospel-Centered Woman* (blog), last accessed January 8, 2016, http://gospelcenteredwoman.com/complementarian-organizations-and-where-women-belong/ (emphasis in original).

most often a Friday night and Saturday gig. But sometimes the women have their retreats from Friday through Sunday. I respectfully decline speaking at or attending the Sunday portion of the retreat, saying that I cannot give them what their own pastor can in the Sunday service. You cannot simply swap a women's retreat for a worship service. Even though we have prayer, singing of hymns and praise, and theological teaching, they are not the same. And, as blessed as I am to spend time with all the wonderful women I meet from different churches in the retreat setting, on Sunday I need to hear the preached Word in the context where God has promised to bless us in Christ. It always shocks me that the elders of a church would approve of their women's ministry having their own replacement service on Sunday morning, separate from the rest of the church body and the elements of proper worship. In this situation, it seems that we are erring on the side of giving women the appearance of the authoritative office in the church so that we can give them an extra retreat day. We are sometimes being protective of the wrong things when it comes to women in both the church and the parachurch.

When it comes to parachurch conferences, it would make sense to ask both men and women who are qualified to speak on the topic at hand. The men will probably still hold a majority of the speaking engagements, as many pastors will be well qualified and there are more men than women holding higher degrees in theology. But there are certainly educated women. And, if a conference is inviting authors to speak, why not see what women have written on the topics at hand as well? For instance, I attended a conference on marriage at which all the speakers were men. This baffles me, because women have a lot to contribute on this topic! Not surprisingly, there were not many women attending the conference.

There are many opportunities for laypeople at parachurch

conferences. Church officers can benefit from the perspective of informed, experienced laypeople who are living a life of faith and obedience in the world outside the church. The parachurch world is made up of many laypeople—both men and women—in Christian publishing, schools, and other organizations, who work hard to provide resources and services that are helpful to the church. We gain when both women and men are involved in conference speaking, workshops, and panel discussions. And by doing this, we are functioning well as a parachurch, keeping these events distinct from the worship service and therefore valuing its specific mission and ecclesiology.

To the Church Officers

How can you encourage mutual learning between the men and the women in your church that trickles down from the ministry of Word and sacrament? There are big things you can do that will send a message, but often it's the little things that can help to shape our thinking in these areas as well. For instance, how often do you quote from women authors, or even from something a woman said to you in conversation that made you stop and think? The writers of Scripture did; so can you.

Is the culture in your church one that takes women's contributions seriously in all areas of theology, not just on the roles of wife and mother or other women's issues? When women in the church begin feeling fragmented or stereotyped, they can easily become restless and look somewhere else for community and participation.[22] Orthodox churches want to

---

22. For further discussion, see Natalie Brand, *Complementarian Spirituality: Reformed Women and Union with Christ* (Eugene, OR: Wipf & Stock, 2013), 115–16.

respond biblically to much of the teaching in the feminist movement today, but it also helps to ask why that movement even began. Women, like all people, are likely to rebel when they are marginalized. The case of Anne Hutchinson is a good illustration. Would things have been different if there had been a better engagement between the women and the church officers at that time? Would she have claimed special revelation from God if her own words had carried more weight? Would she have held to the familism that she was charged with, or had the antinomian leanings that she is accused of today, if she hadn't been in such opposition to the authority of the Puritan church? Back then, women had to sit on the opposite side of the church from men. Anne's meetings in her home seem like a reasonable reaction to the segregation in the church.[23] There she taught and learned without the oversight and engagement of the elders. While we have come a long way, there are some parallels still in women's ministry. If there were better engagement between women and church officers, maybe fewer women would be exposed to faulty doctrines in the studies they participate in. If women felt that their input was valued, their questions were taken seriously, and they were connected to the whole church community, maybe they would be less likely to sacrifice orthodoxy for community. Of course, there will always be false teachers, error, and even just poor theology promoted in our churches. And there will always be rebellious women—and men. But let's challenge the women in their teaching roles, just as much as we would the men, with both positive encouragement and careful, thoughtful critique.

What are your thoughts on the place of women in parachurch conferences? There seems to be little talk about

23. See Williams, *Divine Rebel*, 95.

this—just a few articles in the blogosphere.[24] One blogger compares parachurch conferences to little kids playing house. He says, "The word 'church' (ekklesia) has at least two dimensions to it. It has both a functional component, 'assembling', and an ontological aspect, 'new covenant people.'"[25] It's clear that the ontological status of a parachurch conference is not the same as that of a church. But Ryan Shelton says that when Christians assemble in a parachurch setting, they are performing one aspect of the functional component of the church— assembling—even though they are clearly not the church. Shelton says that if we are going to "play church," then we should expect it to look like church. He explains that of course we are going to have to mimic some of the principles that the apostles gave to the church, just as children mimic household roles when they play house.

But why would we want to be compared to children playing house? Surely we would want the parachurch to function in a more mature manner than playing church! The parachurch exists to come alongside the church as an advocate, dare I say an ally, providing helpful resources and avenues to serve. They shouldn't do that by mimicking the church. That creates all kinds of confusion, particularly with regard to which aspects are essential to mimic (i.e., authority) and which parts may be ignored (i.e., sacraments). What do you think about the effect that this has on the local church and its officers? Can't a conference just be a conference?

There's a lot to think about on this topic, and there's no easy formula we can all follow here. We have clear principles

---

24. We've also done a podcast on it at Carl Trueman, Todd Pruitt, and Aimee Byrd, "Pink Theology," *Mortification of Spin*, Alliance of Confessing Evangelicals, podcast audio, November 11, 2015, http://www.alliancenet.org/mos/podcast /38644.

25. Ryan David Shelton, "Playing House & Playing Church," *Ryan David Shelton* (blog), April 22, 2015, http://ryandavidshelton.com/2015/04/22/playing-house/.

for the worship service and church government in Scripture. But where does something like Sunday school fit in? Small groups? Christian education? What programs or initiatives does your church have in these areas, and what roles do women play in them?

Questions for Reflection and Discussion

1. To recap and highlight the main point, what is the difference between a pastor preaching and a man or woman teaching God's Word outside of a worship service?

2. What is your stance on men learning from women? Has it been challenged or confirmed at all by this chapter? Are there some points on which you disagree with me? Explain.

3. Do you think that Priscilla's name being placed before Aquila's in Scripture threatened his manhood? How about her tent-making skills and discernment? What can their example teach us about gender roles in the home, in the church, and in vocations?

4. How does Hannah's prayer give us a glimpse of Israel's future deliverance from its enemies as we see its fulfillment through the leadership of her son, and how does it also point to an even greater salvation of God's people through his Son?

5. How can ordinary people like us be comforted by the words in the prayers of Hannah and Mary?

6. What does the lack of critique of the content of women's teaching reveal about how seriously we take it? Do you think we should critique women's teaching differently than we do men's?

7. *Church officers*, here are some of the questions addressed to you in this chapter: How can you encourage mutual

learning between the men and the women in your church that trickles down from the ministry of Word and sacrament? How often do you quote from women authors—or even from something a woman said to you in conversation that made you stop and think? Is the culture in your church one that takes the women's contributions seriously in all areas of theology, not just with respect to the roles of wife and mother or other women's issues? What are your thoughts on the place of women in parachurch conferences?

WHAT SHOULD WE
BE DOING THEN?

My husband drops our thirteen-year-old daughter off at school every morning on his way to work. Matt enjoys this morning time much more than Zaidee does, however. You see, Zaidee owns her role as middle child like a boss. You know what I'm talking about. She's the one who likes to ruffle everyone's feathers (which is an apt metaphor, since we are Byrds) in her own playful, yet abrasive way. But middle school has a way of homing in on one's inhibitions, and Matt capitalizes on our poor daughter's vulnerability when he drops her off in the morning. All of a sudden, the same girl who plays her music too loud in the house and doesn't think much before she speaks around her brother and sister is conservative and premeditative at 7:30 a.m. "Dad, turn down the radio, and don't say *anything* when I get out!" At this point, Zaidee knows the futility of her words and can sense the sinister intent behind his obliging smile. Matt likes to wait for her to be a little on her way, thinking that she may just make it into the building with her dignity, before rolling down the passenger window and playing the role of the cheesy dad shouting out his loving good-byes. My favorite send-off of Matt's is "Live, laugh, love!"

Matt does something brilliant there. In his playful mission to remind our daughter that she's worth more than a self-important, but fragile, middle-school ego, he echoes a popular phrase of convictions that used to mean something but now have been commoditized and trivialized. These words are on coffee mugs, journals, calendars, tattoos, and dining room walls. Now, instead of conveying enlightening convictions about life—you know, advice that a father could give to his daughter—they just sound cheesy.

And that is a shame. The woman who first penned these words for inspiration would not recognize them as they are used today. They come from a poem, "Success," that Bessie Anderson Stanley wrote in 1904 as the winning entry in a *Brown Book Magazine* contest.

He has achieved success
who has lived well,
laughed often, and loved much;

who has enjoyed the trust of
pure women,

the respect of intelligent men and
the love of little children;

who has filled his niche and accomplished his task;

who has left the world better than he found it
whether by an improved poppy,
a perfect poem or a rescued soul;

who has never lacked appreciation of Earth's beauty
or failed to express it;

who has always looked for the best in others and
given them the best he had;

whose life was an inspiration;
whose memory a benediction.[1]

As you can see, there was much more conviction behind these three words than whatever the modern consumer's version of living, laughing, and loving may be. These words express doctrine in an artful, authentic way. The poem also reveals some of the ideals and movements of that time period, when women were believed to have moral authority, purity being their greatest currency, and men believed to be the primary bearers of intellect.[2] Nonetheless, this poem gives us a context in which to understand the author's actual meaning for living well, laughing often, and loving much.

Matt's funny send-off to Zaidee also illustrates one of the points of this book. Most of us women who get together for Bible studies and book studies do it because we have convictions about being Christian women in our day. Those of us who teach want to share our convictions for the benefit of the church. And yet we can easily get caught up in the personalities and images attached to these messages, all the while losing the very substance of our convictions.

Convictions are a good thing. All you have to do is scroll

---

1. For the story of the poem, told by Stanley's great-granddaughter, see Robin Olsen, "Truth behind 'Success,'" Robin's Web, August 31, 2001, http://www.robins web.com/truth_behind_success.html.

2. See Sara Moslener, *Virgin Nation: Sexual Purity and American Adolescence* (New York: Oxford University Press, 2015).

through a Twitter or Facebook feed to see many strong beliefs held by your friends in the cyber world. Some of these convictions are well intended but uninformed. Many Christians fall into this category. We need to be careful not to be led by our sentiments to the detriment of our competency in God's Word. And so one thing we should be doing is taking our theology seriously.

Doctrine and life aren't two separate categories. Fred Zaspel persuades the reader of this in his biography *Warfield on the Christian Life*: "For Warfield theology is not merely some added, optional dimension to the Christian life: it is the very stuff of Christian living."[3] Benjamin B. Warfield contended in his writings that if you are indifferent to Christian doctrine, then you are indifferent to Christianity. What is a confession of hope without content? "Warfield argues that in this sense Christianity aims first at the mind. In terms of both evangelism and Christian growth Christianity offers first a message, a word from God—that is, doctrine."[4]

And yet Facebook posts and casual conversations show that many strongly held convictions are shaped by fear, sentimentality, or some other emotional appeal. Sure, emotions are important, but we have wrongly given them the steering wheel. For example, it is easy to see the appeal of reading about things like gratitude or even suffering, and that sounds pretty good so far. But these themes can be romanticized to the point where we become undiscerning and ignore the fact that mysticism is driving the car—I mean, book.

We need to recognize that our sentimentality is being exploited and our faith is being trivialized. In his book *Homespun Gospel*, Todd Brenneman reasons, "It is not theologians or

---

3. Fred G. Zaspel, *Warfield on the Christian Life* (Wheaton, IL: Crossway, 2012), 37.
4. Ibid., 39.

seminary professors who are making the most impact in evangelicalism. It is these personable ministers who have cultivated publishing and product empires through their emotional appeals."[5] Have we lost the ability to distinguish truth from error in what we are reading because the authors appeal so well to our sentimentality? If a message is to be taken seriously, then it probably shouldn't be reduced to being marketed on dollar store trinkets and wind chimes.

This is a real problem. But it isn't all that new (well, maybe the wind chimes are). Warfield implored Christians to put their minds back in the driver's seat, and Zaspel expands upon it so well:

> The character of our theology will shape the character of our religion, and any defective view of God's character will be reflected in the soul and the peace of conscience we are meant to enjoy. If we have no doctrine, we have no Christianity. If we have scanty doctrine, we have scanty Christianity. If we have profoundly informed convictions, we will have a solid and substantial Christianity.[6]

Zaspel exhorts us to be guided by the truth found in God's Word. Let's hold informed convictions. Proper theology—what God's Word reveals about his person and his work—comes first. Let that drive our talk and shape our emotions. If we let sentimentality drive the car, theology becomes a warped add-on and we find ourselves riding down the wrong path—one littered with wind chimes.

Those of us who are disgusted by the exploitation of our sentiments in the Christian bookstore may be blind to the

---

5. Todd M. Brenneman, *Homespun Gospel: The Triumph of Sentimentality in Contemporary American Evangelicalism* (New York: Oxford University Press, 2014), 3.

6. Zaspel, *Warfield on the Christian Life*, 48.

same thing happening within our own parachurch and reading circles. Our empathies can cloud our discernment even on noble topics that we should want to understand and model well, such as social justice, biblical womanhood, or prayer. As necessary allies in the church and in our homes, we need to have clear eyes that will not settle for less than God's truth in our relationships, learning, influencing, and teaching.

Church Officers and Women, Listen Up

We should be able to turn to our local churches here. The church is the ambassador of the gospel. One mission of a household is to hand down its convictions to the next generation. We want churches full of competent women who can discern God's Word well. Offering regular classes on the doctrine of Scripture, the attributes of God, the doctrines of grace, and the orthodox creeds and confessions of the church is a great way to invest in all the members of the church, not only the women. Whether this is done as a coed endeavor or one in which women study together exclusively, it is wise to incorporate women teachers who can mentor others to teach as well. Such classes should be continually offered in a church, because we anticipate new members who also need to build their convictions on the truth. Hopefully, the same types of people who revealed how unbiblical their well-intended convictions are in the LifeWay survey I mentioned in chapter 2 will make their way into our churches. Maybe it will be because one of the women in the church began having a positive and challenging influence on them.

Church membership classes often present good opportunities to teach the confessions of the church. But these are truths that need repeating. It's not enough that we learned some principles of God's Word fifteen years ago and know that our notes must be stashed away somewhere. As we grow in the church, we need to build on these basic truths so that we know them well enough to teach them ourselves (see Heb. 5:12). We need to be able to apply these truths to our different circumstances and theological questions about life. It's one thing to learn the information, but it's another to rehearse it, prayerfully meditate on it, and actively apply it to our everyday lives.

So, just to get really practical, what would it look like for a classroom discussion to pair teaching on some of our basic doctrines together with how those doctrines relate to personal challenges that many Christians encounter? We could explore "God's sovereignty and our anxieties," "the sufficiency of Scripture and how to know if I'm in God's will," "the image of God and biblical womanhood," "the resurrection and living as a new creation," or "true repentance and our spiritual growth." Those would be some interesting discussions—difficult ones even. There are great books written on some of these topics that could be used as resources. Let's bring these conversations into the church, where we can learn how our doctrines shape some of the meaningful questions that we are asking in our everyday lives. Let's sharpen our theology under the guidance of those who are responsible shepherds of our souls! These are just some of the practical ways we can be investing in our women and equipping them to disciple others.

The Total Christ

So much attention has been placed on the offices of the church, household roles, and biblical womanhood and manhood that an overarching truth has been neglected. While we love to talk about union with Christ when we talk about our salvation, it seems to be used less often as a basis for discussing our relationships and church life. Natalie Brand has written on Reformed women and union with Christ. In discussing the role of the sacraments, she describes them as "a means of inserting the believer into the total Christ, that is, Christ and his church."[7] That statement made me close her book and pause for a moment. It seemed brazen to refer to Christ's relationship with his church as the "total Christ."

It can be difficult to handle the tension between God's transcendence and his immanent presence with us in Christ. Out of fear of trying to make him too much like me, I prefer focusing on his transcendence. So a statement like that was jolting, even sending up a red flag. And yet I stopped and thought about what it would mean. I can't think of myself without thinking of Christ. I can't. My identity is totally wrapped up in my being *in Christ*. And, in gratitude for my salvation and awareness of my complete unworthiness for such grace, I have never allowed myself to think of the other side of it.

Theologians often refer to the biblical notion of the church as the bride of Christ when illustrating our union with him. I've been married for over nineteen years. It's been long enough now that this identity has sunk into my identity. I am Matt's wife. When absent from him, I still represent him. It's part of my status, one that was strange to get used to at first, as exciting as it was. My name changed. My home changed. I would never think of myself without considering how my thoughts and actions affected my husband, whom I love dearly.

And although I love to reckon myself part of the church, Christ's bride, when I think of the "total Christ" I think of the divine Trinity, not so much his relationship with the church. I talk about the absolute privilege that it is for me to enjoy

---

7. Natalie Brand, *Complementarian Spirituality: Reformed Women and Union with Christ* (Eugene, OR: Wipf & Stock, 2013), 52.

Christ himself and all his blessings. Sure, I say it all the time. I say it without allowing myself to personalize it fully. But if Jesus is constantly interceding on behalf of his church to the Father, then we are foremost on his agenda all the time! If the covenant of redemption was made in eternity, then we are a perpetual part of Christ.[8]

Brand quotes the work of many Reformed theologians on the union of Christ, but what she includes from Herman Bavinck made me want to go directly to the source and read him further. He uses some similar language in his teaching on Christ's exaltation and our union with him. He teaches that Christ is now filling the church with himself, which is the fullness of God.

> As the church does not exist apart from Christ, so Christ does not exist without the church. He is "the head over all things" (Eph. 1:22; Col. 1:18), and the church is the body . . . formed from him and from him receives its growth (Eph. 4:16; Col. 2:19), thus growing to maturity "to the measure of the full stature of Christ" (Eph. 4:13). The union between Christ and the church is as close as that between the vine and the branches, between bridegroom and bride, husband and wife, cornerstone and building. *Together with him it can be called the one Christ* (1 Cor. 12:12). It is to perfect the church that he is exalted to the Father's right hand.[9]

Christ has united himself in such a way to his church that we can be called the total Christ, or the one Christ! And at this very moment he is interceding on our behalf to accomplish

---

8. See Ps. 110; Rom. 8:34; Heb. 7:25; 9:24; 1 John 2:1.
9. Herman Bavinck, *Reformed Dogmatics*, vol. 3, *Sin and Salvation in Christ*, ed. John Bolt, trans. John Vriend (Grand Rapids: Baker Academic, 2006), 474 (emphasis added).

his work of transforming us into his own likeness. All of us! This should always be on the forefront of our minds as we serve together. While church office and gender distinction are important, we need to make sure that we relate to one another according to this great truth. We love to say that men and women are equal in God's image, but do we act on that basis?

And yet, as I am using our union with Christ as a foundation for relationships and growth in God's church, please do not mistake that for ignoring his transcendence. Jesus volunteered himself to enter into union with us. And he pursued us; we did not pursue him. He has no dependence on his creation and could have existed for eternity in righteousness without us. But we cannot exist for a second, much less for eternity, without him. He sustains and upholds all things! Every bit of our righteousness is dependent upon Jesus. But he made a covenant to unite himself with his beloved as the Bridegroom. In modern-day language, we may even say that he's obsessed with us. It's almost inconceivable. We will inherit Christ's own inheritance in glory. Everything of his will be ours—though not his essence, for we are created beings and he is God. But he has given us his very Spirit. And we are united to him in matrimony so that we are considered one flesh. Christ became man so that we may be like him! We are joined to him, and he is joined to us!

A Woman's Unique Contribution

And yet we wait. Man, is waiting tough! Here we are, betrothed to Christ, new creations, regenerated and united to him by the work of the Holy Spirit, waiting for that great day of consummation. The already of our new life in Christ and the not yet of its consummation are described as being in tension. Our future state can seem unattainable when we compare our spiritual maturity now to what we will be in our perfected state of glorification. And yet we are declared justified and told to strive for that holiness as we focus our eyes on Christ and rest our assurance on his promises and his work. You may have no desire to run a marathon on this earth, but that is the analogy that we are given for perseverance in the Christian life. This is our charge:

> Therefore, since we are surrounded by so great a cloud of witnesses, let us also lay aside every weight, and sin which clings so closely, and let us run with endurance the race that is set before us, looking to Jesus, the founder and perfecter of our faith, who for the joy that was set before him endured the cross, despising the shame, and is seated at the right hand of the throne of God. (Heb. 12:1–2)

Thankfully, we are to set our eyes on Christ, who will get us to the end. And we do not run the race alone but run it with the whole covenant community. I have no desire to run an actual marathon. But, if I do run at all, the finish line motivates me to continue. Our goal in perseverance is eternal life with Christ Jesus in holy, resurrected bodies in the new heavens and the new earth. Our goal is the great feast of consummation as we behold Christ in all his glory. So how does that affect the way that we run?

To put it another way, what do you think our relationships and service to one another will be like in the new heavens and the new earth in our resurrected bodies? And since we will all together be the bride of Christ, what will be the significance of our gender? I'm with C. S. Lewis on this one. Our sexuality is very important and has eternal value. And, although we will no longer marry or give birth, we will function better within our sexuality there than we ever did here. Lewis suggests, "Sexuality is the instrument both of virginity and of conjugal virtue; neither men nor women will be asked to throw away weapons they have used victoriously."[10] While we all are made in the image of God and the whole church is united to Christ, we have some unique roles now as men and women. How can we grow and mature as a church with an eschatological view in mind?

Along with being called the bride of Christ, the church refers to its members as brothers and sisters. Men will never be sisters, and women will never be brothers. These roles are unique to our genders. I have been blessed with biological siblings, for whom I have great love. My close relationship with them has helped me to understand my role as a sister in God's household. I like to playfully advise single women to go for the men who grew up with sisters. Sisters really help to prepare our brothers for marriage to a woman.[11] And while men will never be sisters, they do share with us in the role of Christ's bride. Hopefully we are helping to prepare our brothers for this role as we await his return.

You see, we aren't to wait passively for Christ's return. We are to be active. We have the illustration of a marathon for the Christian life of faith and obedience. And in 1966 Roberta Gibbs showed the world that, despite stereotypes at the time, women can be great marathon runners too (although she had to disguise herself as a man to do it).[12]

---

10. C. S. Lewis, *Miracles* (New York: Collier Books, 1960), 160.

11. I shamelessly take part of the credit for my brother's gentlemanly qualities. Unfortunately for him, he's learned much of his patience by being sandwiched between two crazy sisters.

12. See Ellen Mandeville, "Male and Female He Created Them," Christ & Pop Culture, December 7, 2015, http://christandpopculture.com/male-and-female-he -created-them/, where Roberta Gibbs is used as an illustration for gender paradigms in the church.

The Waiting Room

As a mom, I have developed a fondness for waiting rooms. My whole perspective has changed. I've come to look at them as special places where I am not allowed to do anything—except for one of my favorite things. What? The doctor is running forty-five minutes behind? Fantastic! I will just sit in this chair reading my book, unbothered. Whatever responsibilities I need to attend to will have to wait, because I have to wait—with a book. It's like I'm being forced to do what I long for. There's no guilt involved, no dirty dishes looming over me, no phone calls to make, no arguments to adjudicate. It's very liberating to be in the waiting room.

Unfortunately, I am not so patient when God keeps me waiting. In those times, I find myself a bit anxious, wondering what I am supposed to do while I am waiting. How long will this waiting take? Why do I have to wait? I become that pesky kid in the backseat repeating, "Are we there yet?" Of course, despite my ignorance, God has a purpose in insisting on my waiting. He is preparing my mind and heart, as well as his providential circumstances.

Many times in the Bible, God makes his people wait. Often it is for a very long time. Did you know there was a waiting room in Scripture? Well, kind of, anyway. We'll use it for my little metaphor. I'm talking about the command that Jesus gave his disciples right before his ascension. He told them not to leave Jerusalem, but to stay there and wait for the promise of the Holy Spirit (see Acts 1:4–5). Thankfully, this wouldn't be an Abraham-needing-an-heir kind of wait or a Jacob-pining-for-Rachel kind of wait. Jesus assured them that the promised Spirit would come "not many days from now," which ended up being ten days. So there they were, talking face-to-face with Jesus Christ, who had just been resurrected from the dead. He was about to leave, and as their Lord he commanded them to wait. Their reply went something like, "Are we there yet?" Well, not in those exact words, but basically they revealed just how clueless they still were about God's kingdom (see Acts 1:6). They were still thinking much too narrowly about God's plan of salvation and the dimensions of his kingdom.

Why did Christ make them wait? Obviously they still weren't "ripe," as Calvin puts it in his commentary. He makes some other good points about their being made to wait. Making the apostles wait sharpened their desire and helped them to better realize the greatness of the office they were assigned. Calvin points out that "we must work and rest at the Lord's pleasure alone" and that "we are made partakers of the gifts of God through hope."[13] In bidding us to wait, God is also encouraging us to persevere.

After Jesus told them to go back and wait, he was lifted up to heaven in a cloud. Can you imagine the expressions on their faces? Think about the curious blend of bewilderment and excitement they must have been feeling. Talk about an adrenaline rush! Two angels appeared and basically told them to snap out of it, assuring them that Christ would return in the same way in which he had left.

So off to the waiting room they went. They must have had many questions as they walked the two miles back to Jerusalem. They had just witnessed something miraculous. What was going on? What was this power that they were about to receive? How were they going to be Christ's witnesses? What did he mean by "not many days from now"? We don't get the inside scoop on that conversation. But we do get the news that they obeyed.

---

13. John Calvin, *Commentary upon the Acts of the Apostles*, vol. 1, in *John 12–21, Acts 1–13*, trans. Henry Beveridge, Calvin's Commentaries 18 (repr., Grand Rapids: Baker, 2003), 38–39.

What did they do in the waiting room? "All these with one accord were devoting themselves to prayer, together with the women and Mary the mother of Jesus, and his brothers" (Acts 1:14). They devoted themselves to prayer. They prayed expectantly, persistently, and of one mind. And notice that the women were there. Women were active during the Lord's ministry on earth, and they were also active during the waiting period. How beautiful this verse is, showing men and women praying together for his promised gift of the Holy Spirit. As a result of this, they were led to the business of finding a replacement for Judas. The disciples waited well.

We can apply this to situations in our own lives when the Lord doesn't answer our prayers as soon as we want him to. Waiting is difficult, but it is not passive. It certainly isn't wasted time, either. We can wait with the confidence that, even though we may not be seeing any results, the Lord is producing exactly what he wants in his time. And we can know that it is good because he is good.

But there is also a sense in which we are all waiting. We are all waiting for what the angels told the apostles was sure to happen—that Jesus Christ is going to return in the same manner in which he ascended.

> For our citizenship is in heaven, from which we also eagerly wait for the Savior, the Lord Jesus Christ, who will transform our lowly body that it may be conformed to His glorious body, according to the working by which He is able even to subdue all things to Himself. (Phil. 3:20–21 NKJV)

On that day, all his promises will be made good.

How are we to wait? Eagerly. "To those who eagerly wait for Him He will appear a second time, apart from sin, for salvation" (Heb. 9:28 NKJV). And, during Christ's ministry on earth (including his crucifixion and resurrection), while the disciples waited for his promises in the upper room, and during the missionary work and building of the early church, we see women playing active roles as necessary allies. They were just as eager as the men.

Thankfully, we also have the gift of the Comforter as we eagerly wait for our Bridegroom. He helps us in our prayers and is working to get us ready for that day of which no man knows the time. As we stumble about, trying to live the life that God would have us live in these last days, his Spirit is teaching us how to wait. And that waiting involves some marathon running!

Because We Do Stumble About

So what are we to be doing? We are to recognize that women are created in the image of God as necessary allies to men in carrying out his mission. Because of this, women are to be good theologians with informed convictions. We are to take this call seriously and invest quality time in our theological growth and Bible study within the context of our local church as a foundation to our service and contributions to the church, our families, and society. The church is to recognize this and help to equip competent women as necessary allies. And as we uphold the headship roles in household management, we are to relate to one another on the basis of our unity in Christ. Elders are also to ensure that the mature women in the church can pass down their knowledge to the younger women in the faith, explaining how our doctrine relates to our everyday lives and roles. And yet we stumble as we try to faithfully work this out. We see this in Scripture, we see it in church history, and we are still stumbling about now.

There is no book in the Bible that deals with biblical

womanhood or gender paradigms in the church. There isn't even a chapter written to explain how the woman is to function as an *ezer*. But we do see that life is not good without women, and that with women it is "very good." And God uses the same word, *ezer*, to describe woman that he uses for himself, in many instances in Scripture, to show how he is necessary to Israel's survival.[14] Thus John McKinley states, "God is the ultimate *ezer* to all people in need, but woman is God's provision of a necessary ally to men for the good of both and all people that depend on their synergy."[15] Maybe you are wondering how we go about doing that. McKinley outlines some of the ways in which women function as necessary allies in Scripture and, conversely, in which sin causes them to function as opponents instead:[16]

Women Are Necessary Allies to Men by *Warning Them to Turn Away from Evil.*

We see some valiant examples of this in Scripture. Abigail risked her own life to warn David not to seek revenge on her "worthless" husband, Nabal. David saw the wisdom of her advice and, in heeding it, was saved from "bloodguilt" by leaving Nabal's personal offense against him to the sovereign provision of God (see 1 Sam. 25:1–42). There's the unnamed wise woman who somehow managed to get the attention of David's army as they were battering her city wall to topple it down. She insisted on speaking with the commander, Joab, gave him a strong warning that he should reconsider destroying a city that was so faithful to Israel, and reasoned with him

---

14. See John McKinley, "Necessary Allies: God as *Ezer*, Woman as *Ezer*," lecture, Hilton Atlanta, November 17, 2015, mp3 download, 38:35, http://www.wordmp3 .com/details.aspx?id=20759.

15. Ibid.

16. Ibid., for the following points and most of the Scripture references.

to let her retrieve the man he was really after. She then persuaded the city to cut off Sheba's head and throw it over the wall to Joab. Again, this was not really a job that you would typically imagine a woman doing. She was called wise and certainly persevered as a necessary ally to both David's army and her city (see 2 Sam. 20). Also, the prophetess Deborah warned Barak that if she went to battle with him like he insisted, the glory of victory would go to another woman, not to him (see Judg. 4:1–5:31). And the prophetess Huldah warned Josiah of divine judgment on the people for breaking God's covenant, yet assured him that it would be delayed until after his lifetime, since he had repented and humbled himself before God when he heard the Scriptures read (see 2 Chron. 34:22–28).

In contrast, we have some examples in Scripture of women who were opponents to men by not warning them to turn away from evil. Our most notorious one is the first lady herself, of course. She did not warn Adam regarding her evil conversation partner. And interestingly, when Israel was finally going to enter the Promised Land, Achan committed the same sin that Adam had committed in Paradise. After the Lord had given specific instructions for their victory at Jericho, Achan took and hid for himself some of the devoted things that were to be put in God's treasury. When God singled out his family for judgment, Achan finally confessed with the language that we see in Genesis. First he *saw* the treasures, then he coveted them, and then he *took* them (see Josh. 7:21; cf. Gen. 3:6). Achan was stoned and burnt alive in front of (or along with) his sons and daughters; his sin had already caused the Lord's anger to burn against the entire covenant community. But we do not read any mention of Achan's wife, as we do of Adam's wife. If she had been with him, it would have been impossible for her not to notice a hole dug in their tent with treasure in it. A woman knows these things. Either he no longer had a wife, thus lacking the blessing of an ally to warn him, or she did know and, as his opponent, did not warn him in his sin. If he had had a loving wife warning him of the evil of his sin, maybe things would have been different. Much later, at the beginning of the early church, Sapphira knew that her husband kept back some of the profit from the sale of their property and presented money to the apostles as if it were all he had made—not because there was a command for him to do so, but just so that he would appear as generous as Barnabas. Rather than warning Ananias that Satan was filling his heart with the desire to lie, she participated in the lie, and they were both struck dead (see Acts 5:1–11).

Women Are Necessary Allies to Men *as Cobelligerents against Evil Enemies.*

When enemies come near, we are to align ourselves, combining forces with our brothers to rally against it. Again, Deborah and the woman who gave Joab the head of Sheba are great examples. The discerning Abigail was also belligerent against her wicked husband's refusal to care for David and his men when she bravely brought them ample food and wine, along with offering her deepest apologies and wisdom to David. She then joined him once the Lord avenged Nabal. The book of Esther reveals a woman's incredible faith and godly tenacity in defending her people as a cobelligerent with Mordecai against the evil plans of Haman. And, as courageous as Esther was, we see it as her showing faithfulness to her own people as a Jew. But Rahab demonstrated valiant resolve as a cobelligerent with Israel against her own people, hiding two spies in her home at her own risk. Rahab, a prostitute, recognized the Lord's work and wanted to join in! So she helped the spies to escape, after they promised that they would remember her when the Lord gave them the land (see Josh. 2).

By contrast, Lot's wife did not join her husband in obedience to the angels' words as they fled Sodom. Rather than hating the wickedness that had consumed their city, she waivered. While Lot obediently ran away from evil, his wife looked back and fell under the judgment of the Lord. This of course affected Lot immediately, as he was left with two daughters who took advantage of him, producing progeny that become Israel's enemies (see Gen. 19). And who can forget Delilah, the woman who seduced Samson in order to find out the secret of his strength and betray him to his enemies, the Philistines, for a payoff (see Judg. 16)? Israel has some wicked women in its royal history, such as Maacah and Athaliah, who were opponents of godliness rather than cobelligerents against evil.

Women Serve as Necessary Allies by *Mediating the Word of the Lord.*

There are many women in Scripture who play a prophetic role, conveying God's word. Miriam, the prophetess, tambourine in hand, led the women of Israel to sing, after they crossed the Red Sea, "Sing to the LORD, for he has triumphed gloriously; the horse and his rider he has thrown into the sea" (Ex. 15:21). Again, we have Deborah the prophetess as a good example, as well as Huldah's prophecy, Hannah's prayer, and Mary's song of praise. There is Anna, the aged prophetess who testified to the long-awaited arrival of the Messiah (see Luke 2:36–38). Phillip's four daughters prophesied (see Acts 21:9). Women announced the resurrection of Jesus, women prophesied in Corinth (see 1 Cor. 11:5), and Priscilla informed Apollos about the gospel.

The gift of prophecy has not continued in this age of the church, as the canon is closed and we have God's final word spoken to us in these last days (see Heb. 1:1–2). But since women play a prophetic role throughout Scripture, we do continue to discern, encourage, and build up by speaking God's revealed word in Scripture. In fact, this is a vital aspect of functioning as necessary allies. And it is foundational to our next point.

Women Serve as Necessary Allies by *Giving Wise Instruction and Counsel.*

We see certain women in Scripture pointed out for their wisdom. Wisdom is portrayed with a feminine metaphor in Proverbs, and we see verses such as "Say to wisdom, 'You are my sister,' and call insight your intimate friend" (Prov. 7:4). Women aren't the only possessors of wisdom, but they can offer wisdom from a different perspective than men can, making us valuable to one another. This kind of teaching and counsel from women to men is valued in Scripture. McKinley notes that women are exceptionally nurturing and compassionate in relationships in the home and in the church. He suggests that, since men are also called to be nurturing and compassionate, they learn wisdom in this important area from the women they know. Obviously women are going to be better at teaching women to be wives and mothers, and Paul sets this up as pastoral advice for the church in Crete (see Titus 2:3–5). It's important to establish this kind of mentoring through which women in the church can teach what is good, to the benefit of the whole body of Christ. And again, Priscilla shines bright as a necessary ally in wisdom. McKinley highlights the importance of Luke's mentioning of her, as it connects to Paul's teaching elsewhere in Scripture

> that women and men taught each other in the churches at the level of instruction and counsel, which [he] take[s] to be different from authoritative teaching done by elders in the church. When women are excluded from contributing

instruction and counsel to men, the necessary allies are cut off from giving what God made them to be, and all the people suffer losses as a result.[17]

We also find folly personified as a woman, misleading with her lies that lead to death (see Prov. 9:13–18). Rather than comforting her husband in the goodness and sustenance of the Lord, Job's wife foolishly urged him to curse God and die (see Job 2:9). We also see examples of both wisdom and folly in the queen mothers of Israel in the Old Testament.

Women Serve as Necessary Allies by *Collaboration in Service to Others*.

Men and women worship together, and they also serve together as an outworking of the ministry of Word and sacrament. Strengths of both men and women are needed for carrying out God's mission in the church. The ideal woman in Proverbs 31 is praised for her valuable work and contribution in the household and in society. Women served at the doorway of the tent of meeting (see Ex. 38:8). Miriam collaborated in leading the people of Israel out of Egypt. Wealthy women funded Jesus' mission and traveled with him and his disciples as part of his ministry team. McKinley wonders if their function was similar to the work that Miriam did for Moses and Aaron. Clearly, God appointed women to perform vital services during these special periods of redemptive history. In the early church, prominent women opened their homes to host churches, and others provided hospitality to evangelists. There is debate over whether women deacons served the churches—particularly Phoebe, Paul's *prostatis* and deliverer of his epistle to the Romans. Women served in ministry

17. Ibid.

teams with their husbands, and Paul honored and sent greetings to Euodia, Syntyche, Nympha, Phoebe, Priscilla, Mary, Persis, Tryphaena, Tryphosa, and Junia as coworkers in the gospel. Even the widows played an important role of service to the church. Women collaborated in service in the home, the church, and the world.

Women Serve as Necessary Allies by *Responding to God as Examples of Faithfulness.*

Women have a more experiential knowledge to draw from when it comes to being the bride of Christ. However, I'm not entirely on board with all the reasoning that McKinley gives. He points to women as models of responsiveness to God in a "receptive mode," waiting for the groom to take the initiative. I'm not quite comfortable with describing a bride's role on earth that way. We have the example of Naomi and Ruth taking the initiative to set the Boaz relationship in motion (see Ruth 3). I am sensitive to this kind of language because I have seen it used by abusers in the home and the church. Scripture gives us plenty of examples of active, initiating women, and even of providers.

And yet, my caution reveals an obvious truth: men are physically stronger than women. This does affect the way in which we relate to one another. Women can respond to this truth as doormats, as manipulators, or as competent lovers and friends. Our competence will direct whether we need to warn, encourage, serve, sharpen, flee, fight, or collaborate. God is of course all-powerful. McKinley says, "The identity of the church as the bride of Christ emphasizes the idea that, to God, we're all feminine."[18] Although men and women often fail, God is the faithful and good groom. Women are allies to

18. Ibid.

men when we model competent response to God's initiative. McKinley points to the devotion of Rahab, Deborah, Ruth, Esther, Mary, Elizabeth, the women who stayed at the cross and returned to the tomb, the women at Pentecost, Lydia, and even the women instructed to try to win over their unbelieving husbands by their "respectful and pure conduct" (1 Peter 3:2). We should all be strengthened by dependence on God's Word in all of our relationships, but women have had to faithfully depend on that in ways that are unique from men, given our physical differences, our history in society, and our call to godly submission to our husbands.

Women Serve as Necessary Allies by *Influencing Men from a Gift of Empathy and Relatedness*.

There are of course exceptions to this, but women as a whole tend to have giftedness in intuition, empathy, relationship, and emotional intelligence. We see God's wisdom in gifting us this way to prepare many women for the nurturing, life-providing, and attentive attributes that a mother will need. But these tendencies are not only for motherhood; they are also for sisterhood. It's important to recognize that, although neither Jesus nor Paul were married men, they had close relationships with women as allies in their ministry. I won't repeat the many examples already given in this book that show the contribution that these women made to their ministry and the relational value of their interactions. These women added a richness to their relationships that would have been diminished if they weren't included.

How can we take these principles, along with the many examples in Scripture of competent women serving as necessary allies, and apply them to our relationships in God's household now? Women, do we warn others to turn away from evil, or are we complacent? Do we prefer gossip to godly confrontation?

Do we serve alongside the men as cobelligerents against evil, or do we leave all the dirty work to them? Or, worse, are we the ones stirring the pot? Are we steeped enough in God's Word so that we can provide wisdom, encouragement, and counsel from it? Are we trained in discernment to distinguish godly fruit from counterfeit lies? Do people seek us out for wisdom? Do we offer our resources and time when we see a need? Do we respond in faith to God's calling, or are we irritated every time it seems to interfere with our own agenda? Are we sharpening our gifts of empathy and relational connectedness by the truth of God's Word, or are we letting our emotions take the lead?

What Does It Mean to Be Necessary Allies?

We are crucial partners in carrying out God's mission to the world. What do we do, then, with that honor and responsibility? This is God's plan. He has made man and woman in his image. He has united all his people in Christ so that we are to be thought of as one with him. He has given us new life through his Holy Spirit and through the ministry of Word and sacrament. And he intends for us to be friends—brothers and sisters who love and depend on one another as we persevere in the Christian life of faith and obedience, actively serving as we wait for our Bridegroom. He wants us to do this because evil is very real and our flesh is weak. As we strive together to live in holiness and to spread the gospel to an unbelieving world, we continue to struggle with our sinful desires and actions. We need collaborators in our mission, people who offer us the same grace that they have received, without lowering our standards of holiness. We need cobelligerents against evil, people who strengthen us where we are weak and sharpen the gifts that we have. We need richness in our relationships that model the richness we have in Christ. God hasn't given us merely coworkers in the work of the gospel but a spiritual household with whom to enjoy him together.

The way we relate to each other now as crucial partners will transfer into the eternal covenantal community when we are Christ's bride in the new heavens and the new earth. We will not be resurrected to live an individualistic faith with our Bridegroom. That is not the image of God. So let's model that now. This means that we won't settle for cheesy knock-offs or compartmentalized ministries. Let's step up as necessary allies with our eyes on the finish line. Let's recognize the gift that God has given us in community—teaching, learning, rehearsing, practicing, and exploring the truths he has given us together.

Questions for Reflection and Discussion

1. In your reading, listening to the radio, teaching, social media interaction, and conversation, do you find a lot of appeals for convictions that are shaped by fear, sentimentality, or other emotions that are not rooted in scriptural truths? What would you say is making the most significant impact on your convictions? How informed are your convictions?

2. Do you tend to adapt the same convictions as your favorite leaders without thinking critically through them yourself?

3. If your church offered classes on the doctrine of Scripture and hermeneutics, would you take them? *Pastors and church officers*, what do you think about my suggestions for classes combining important doctrines with our life experiences and troubles?

4. How does your reflection on your union with Christ and the new heavens and new earth affect your view of the

church? How does it affect your perspective on learning, serving, influencing, and teaching?

5. Review the different functions of a necessary ally. Here are some questions from the end of the chapter: How can we take these principles, along with the many examples in Scripture of competent women serving as necessary allies, and apply them to our relationships in God's household now? Do you warn others to turn away from evil, or are you complacent? Do you prefer gossip to godly confrontation? Do you serve alongside the men as cobelligerents against evil, or do you leave all the dirty work to them? Or, worse, are you the one stirring the pot? Are you steeped enough in God's Word so that you can provide wisdom, encouragement, and counsel from it? Are you trained in discernment to distinguish godly fruit from counterfeit lies? Are you someone whom people seek out for wisdom? Do you offer your resources and time when you see a need? Do you respond in faith to God's calling on you, or do you get irritated every time it seems to interfere with your own agenda? Are you sharpening your gifts of empathy and relational connectedness by the truth of God's Word, or are you letting your emotions take the lead?

6. Whom do you know from your church that models this well? How can you learn from her?

PART FOUR

Honing Our Skills

COMPETENT ALLIES

Necessary ally is an honorable title—one that carries a lot of weight and responsibility. This book has made a case for God's designing women as necessary allies and has also taken a hard look at the context of women in the contemporary church, home, and society. No one reading this book wants to be a little woman. But, more than that, we do not want this to be true of *any* women. We've seen that women who do not function as necessary allies often become opponents and enemies of God's mission. In this final section of chapters, we'll shift to a more practical gear and focus on what it takes to grow as necessary allies.

Earlier I mentioned a question that Jesus asked Martha. It is one that I just can't get out of my head. Whenever Martha is mentioned, we tend to think of Jesus telling her that she is anxious and troubled by many things. It is a great teaching point. However, that is not the most confrontational thing he ever said to Martha. Later, when she ran out to meet Jesus after her brother died, Jesus got to the more important matter of declaring who he is and stating the gospel: "I am the resurrection and the life. Whoever believes in me, though he die, yet shall he live, and everyone who lives and believes in me shall never die." Jesus then pressed home even more important words for Martha: "Do you believe this?" (see John 11:17–27). We can easily read these words on a page and see a propositional statement about who Jesus is and a gospel call, properly closed with the element of personal belief and confession—good theology wrapped up with a nice little bow.

But think about the circumstances and the friendship here for a moment. The profound confrontation here is striking. Have you ever asked that question, "Do you believe me?" Imagine the eye contact between the two: Jesus, the Son of God, with his friend and disciple, who is in despair. That question changed everything. His miraculous raising of Lazarus would demonstrate that the answer to this question brings life from death. It's a question not only for Martha but also for all of us. It's a question that reorients our lives now so that we live for the life that is to come. It is a question that moves us from living our lives so as to preserve our own kingdom to living so as to persevere in Christ's kingdom. It is a question that requires the work of the Holy Spirit to open our eyes and ears before we can even see his beautiful grace and majesty, see our own depravity and vanity, and hear this good news.

Jesus' gracious and confrontational question revealed that they weren't talking about the death of her brother anymore; they were talking about Martha's life and death. Jesus is the resurrection and the life. He is the only way to eternal life. Martha's response, "Yes, Lord; I believe that you are the Christ, the Son of God, who is coming into the world" (v. 27), marked the sure death of her own way, her own kingdom building, and her own reasoning, as well as her entrance into a new life that gives everything to the only kingdom that matters. That may not have been the exact moment of her conversion, but there was a clear confrontation and crisis, and her answer solidly professed whom she would serve.

This question is for us too. And by the grace of God, if we answer like Martha, everything changes. We will see that we are called to be necessary allies in God's mission and, therefore, called to be competent women.

In the last chapter, we looked at John McKinley's suggestions on how women serve as necessary allies: by warning men to turn away from evil, as cobelligerents with men against evil enemies, by mediating the Word of the Lord, by collaborating in service to others, by giving wise instruction and counsel, by responding to God as examples of faithfulness, and by influencing men through empathy and relatedness. All of these areas of service require competence. We shouldn't be flailing alongside, making a mediocre contribution; rather, we should be serving well. This takes a lot of conditioning and training.

The Feminist Label

Competent women is a phrase that may sound intimidating at first. Peter tells us to adorn ourselves with "the imperishable beauty of a gentle and quiet spirit" (1 Peter 3:4). If we have the wrong notions of competence, we may think these are opposite poles. Sometimes competent women are thought to be intense, outspoken women who are full of selfish ambition. Perhaps we think of Rosie the Riveter, with her red bandanas and flexing muscles, advertising to all women, "We can do it!" But I am not talking about the self-empowerment message that that iconic picture is now associated with. Unfortunately, instead of being encouraged, many competent women in the church are labeled with the dreaded word *feminist*. It is not helpful to throw this word around carelessly as an insult. Feminism came in different stages, in its latter half adding damaging agendas to the movement's initially commendable and needed work. So the word *feminist* can mean many things.

We should not use it to dismiss capable women who are trying to serve well as necessary allies.

We also need to be careful not to confuse competence with its counterfeits. We who are competent women are not going to have a victim mentality. We are not going to sulk at the slightest perceived offense, and we are going to take responsibility for our actions. How could we possibly wallow in self-pity when Jesus Christ already took on all thoSe offenses, taking the wrath of God for all the injustice and sin of his people, including our own offenses? No, we are going to move on persistently in the path of righteousness, thankful for all that Christ has done, even if the word *feminist* is dropped on us.

On the other hand, a competent ally is not going to act out of a sense of woman power, with the delusional and equally stereotypical mantra, "Anything a man can do a woman can do better." We are going to recognize our interdependence in relationship and not subvert that with our own agendas. That's one thing that went terribly wrong in the feminist movement. The women in the first wave of feminism sacrificed much to oppose the bad treatment of women, wanting to be cobelligerents with men in justice. They stood up against the status quo for the betterment of the church, the family, and society.

Three Traits of a Competent Ally

If women are going to exhibit competence and serve as necessary allies, they will need to be equipped, have resolve, and be discerning.

Be Equipped

First of all, we need to be equipped. Competent women are equipped with an understanding of God's Word. If we are to warn against evil, then we need to be well acquainted with

Good! If we are to mediate the Word of the Lord, then we need to know its content and how to handle it properly. How can we give wise instruction and counsel if we are filling our minds with error and lies? How can we be examples of faithfulness if we feed on a diet of shallow devotionals? Before Jesus asked Martha about her belief, he invited her to join Mary in listening to him. She had to learn the content of her confession of hope before she made it. During their confrontation over Lazarus, Jesus made it clear that he wasn't just the teacher of the truth; he *was* the truth embodied! Jesus communicated specific words and then asked, "Do you believe *this?*" It was not a vague "Do you believe?" The content of what he said was vital. And it was specific.

The problem with the little women mentioned in 2 Timothy 3 wasn't that they were always learning. They were learning from the wrong people and so were never arriving at a knowledge of the truth. We are all learning something. But maybe we have unwittingly let other sources seep in that teach us what we'd rather hear. Let's be always learning, growing in the knowledge of the truth. The only way to do that is to be competent in the Word. We need to know the mission of God if we are going to be allies in it. And God doesn't leave us as isolated individuals to study his Word all alone. No, Scripture is addressed to all of his covenant people, and we have the privilege and responsibility to learn within the covenant community of our local church. The church is called to discipleship. Make sure you are in a church that takes this seriously. Make sure you are worshipping every week, sitting under the preached Word and partaking of the sacraments. Take advantage of the resources available to you there, including Bible studies, training, and biblical teaching materials.

Have Resolve

Secondly, a competent ally has resolve. After being confronted with the truth, we then either align ourselves with it as allies or buck against it as opponents. This is where we lose allies in the race and start stumbling over opponents unwittingly. To have resolve requires sacrifice, and we are in a constant battle as sinful people. Even when it comes to equipping ourselves in the Word, we must resolve to continue in it. We are constantly tempted to preserve our own delusional kingdoms instead of putting in the work it takes to persevere in God's kingdom. Jesus warns us to count the cost before becoming his disciples so that we will not be surprised when we need to lay down our own pride, comfort, time, and sometimes friendships, health, family, and wealth for his kingdom. But if our eyes are on Christ, we will see our great reward, a treasure far greater in value than anything on this earth. He, knowing the cost of our salvation, resolved to become man and suffer in obedience, culminating in the most costly act of all: atoning for our sin on the cross. The cost of discipleship doesn't compare to the reward of serving in his kingdom.

Be Discerning

Thirdly, discernment is vital to our competence. How competent are we in separating the truth from the falsehoods? This is what characterizes the successful necessary allies who we read about in Scripture. There are so many areas in which we need to exercise discernment. And we need to start with ourselves. Are we able to discern our own sinful temptations to stray from godly living? Self-examination can be one of the most difficult areas in which to exercise godly judgment. This is what Jesus called Martha to do when she was upset with her sister and when she was questioning his goodness in delaying his arrival when her brother died. Repentance is a vital part of the Christian life. We will continually fall, but we have an eternal advocate in the Son, who is now at the right hand of the Father and interceding on our behalf. We can go to him in sorrow over our sin and can find forgiveness and the strength to turn away in righteousness (see Heb. 2:14–18; 5:1–10).

Those of us who are married will need to exercise discernment in that relationship. And singles will need great discernment in dating. Abigail is described as a "discerning and beautiful" woman who was married to a "harsh and badly behaved" man (1 Sam. 25:3). She didn't have the same opportunities that single women have today. But, even in our day, many married women have been misled by well-intended but bad advice when it comes to submitting to a husband's ungodly demands. Often women feel paralyzed in these situations because the personal cost seems even worse than taking a stand. And yet Abigail moved with great courage and conviction when her husband refused to extend hospitality to David and his men when they were in need, even after they had been good to him. Because of her character and discernment, one of the young men knew to let her in on the situation. At the risk of her own life and without her husband's knowledge, Abigail quickly gathered ample food and wine for David's men and personally delivered it. She didn't play the victim because her husband was such a worthless man; she took responsibility for her household and reasoned with David, giving him the wise advice not to take vengeance from the Lord's hands. It wasn't about woman power or victimhood. Abigail functioned as a necessary ally in her household and to David; she was established in God's will and resolved to obey it. While we are not to have a disposition of rebellion against our husbands, we are not to submit to ungodliness. We are to be discerning in our marriages. Esther is another good example of this, but we will get to her in our next area of discernment.

We also have a responsibility to be discerning in our society. Government is a sphere, separate from the church, in which we are called to serve with respect under different authorities. However, we don't check our discernment at the door. Esther showed great courage when she spoke for the Jews to her husband, the king, exposing Haman's plot to have them annihilated. Her life was on the line when she approached the inner court without having been summoned. She didn't break that rule without first having the Jews join with her in fasting and prayer for three days. Again we see devotion to God, recognizing the truth from the lies, and a resolve to act as a necessary ally at her own expense.

While Esther's acumen saved her people, Rahab showed great discernment in acting against her own people. When the two spies hid in Rahab's house for refuge, she concealed them on her roof and lied to the officers who came to her house looking for them. Before she helped them escape, she told them that she recognized that they were men from the Lord, the God of heaven and earth. Rahab had been paying attention to the accounts that she had heard about the Israelites. Equipped with this evidence of the true God, she resolved to help these men in carrying out his mission and begged them to rescue her household in return for her act of bravery in keeping them safe (see Josh. 2). Rahab was a prostitute, not a queen or a respectable married woman. The Lord can penetrate through any station we are in and call us to himself. Do you believe this? How does that change your resolve?

We also need to exercise discernment under the preaching of the Word. The Bereans are praised for modeling this responsibility, but we also have the godly example of Priscilla, who recognized the giftedness and calling of Apollos and yet corrected and instructed him in the full knowledge of the gospel. Again, this is not to be done with the attitude of trying to nitpick every word that comes out of your pastor's mouth or to diminish the authority of the preached Word. But we are to be actively engaged with the preached Word and to make sure that we are placing ourselves under solid preaching. We will talk more about this in the last chapter. Discernment is necessary in our relationships and in all of our learning. We are to pursue truth, and that means we have to distinguish truth from error.

Competent with Books

In fact, we should be exercising discernment in everything we do, as there are threats to the truth all the time. Our theology doesn't get checked out when we close our Bibles or walk out of the worship service; it is integral to every part of living as necessary allies. We can't warn others about danger if we are participating in it. We can't give good counsel if we are unable to receive it, and we can't collaborate in service to others if we are inadvertently working against their best interests. One major area in which people check their theology at the door is in what they are reading. Reading is important to our learning, as there is so much good teaching available in books. But, strangely, many people are intimidated by the books that could be good teaching aids for them, and many read without engaging much in the process. How can we increase our learning and grow in our discernment as better readers?

What expectations did you have when you first cracked this book open? Did you have some questions about women and the church that you hoped to have answered? After reading this far, have you been led to even more questions that you are hoping I'm going to get to? Are my arguments persuasive, or are you finding yourself disagreeing with some of the points I have made? These are important questions, not just because they would be helpful for me to hear as an author, but also because they make you a more intelligent reader. That's why we are going to close this chapter by sharpening our critical reading skills with a few practical tips, which will in turn help to sharpen authors and get some edifying conversations going.

I've done a good bit of critique on the books being marketed to Christian women and have exhorted us not to be little women. But, while pinpointing a problem and looking for a solution is important, there is a practical element that is just as vital. If we are to be competent women, then we need to be learners. And reading is a crucial tool for our learning.

Unfortunately, I hear many women confess that they are not readers. The thing is, I know that this isn't true. I see all their Facebook posts. It's not that they don't read; they are reading all the time! It's just that they don't read books. And that is a shame. On the other hand, many women talk about books they are reading that hardly have any real substance at all. The appeal seems to be the personality of the author rather than a desire to learn anything substantial. There are others who take in the teachings of an author without discernment and then just regurgitate her words as if that is the same as having understanding. Still others will read a book as if it's just one opinion among many, collecting an eclectic blend of theology that is meaningless to them. And then there are all those who have great intentions to learn something. They find a book that looks promising, but twenty pages into it they realize that they are in over their head and give up.

So let's address all these situations with some practical and, I hope, encouraging tips for becoming more engaging readers. Most of what I have to say in this section is inspired by *How to Read a Book*, by Mortimer J. Adler and Charles Van Doren.[1] This material will help to hone our reading skills in general. And yet, as faithful Christians, we have some additional

---

1. Mortimer J. Adler and Charles Van Doren, *How to Read a Book* (1940; repr., New York: Simon & Schuster, 1972).

discerning questions we should be asking while we read. The next chapter will provide some additional questions that readers can use to get an accurate overview of an author's message. And then I'll discuss what to do with that information. Should we never read books written by heretical authors? Where is the line of orthodoxy? Are there degrees of theological error and acceptability in evangelical circles?

Why to Read a Book

We read a lot in one day. Unfortunately, it is often in bits and pieces. Our brains are physiologically adapting to the constant notifications and interruptions on our smart phones and computers and to the overwhelming amounts of information available at our fingertips. Our attention spans are shrinking as a result. It's almost understandable when people conclude that they just aren't book readers, even if they may once have hoped that they would be. Many have claimed that we now live in a postliterate society. College professors are complaining that their incoming students have lost the ability to keep up with their reading assignments and lack the ability to write well. So, before getting into how to read a book, we should address why to read a book. Books take us into a completely different category of reading than articles and social media posts can provide. Interestingly, reading *How to Read a Book* further motivated me to read books. Here are five reasons that I've gleaned.

Read books because there is a big difference between gathering information and reading for discovery and understanding. Articles, tweets, and Facebook posts can give us some new information. But we are usually getting this information at a level that is easy to consume and purposefully not challenging to our own understanding. But learning is about more than absorbing new information. Information just gives us the basic building blocks to stretch our understanding and move on to discovery. In order to grow in this way, we need more than a one-thousand-word article. We need to read authors whose writings are over our heads, and to engage in the process of learning from them, so that we can then connect that knowledge to other ideas for new discoveries. It's all very exciting, but the shallow waters of the Internet will never get you there. I will get into this more when we get to the how.

Read books because difficulty is not an excuse to stop. The Internet is physiologically changing our brains. It's becoming harder for us to focus on reading a whole article, much less an entire book. But we don't have to give in to that. We need to exercise our brains to keep the firing paths moving in order to lengthen our attention spans and increase our capacity to think deeply. Just like a constant diet of fast food makes us flabby, so too a constant intake of social media to the neglect of books and thoughtful meditation will make our brains flabby. So if you find it difficult to read more than five pages at a time, or you find yourself falling asleep as soon you crack open a book, that is a sign that you should be putting in the work that it takes to be an active reader. It doesn't mean that books aren't for you. The rewards are always better when we prepare a meal with fresh ingredients than when we are in a hurry and hit the drive-thru.

Read books to join in on the conversation. Authors write books because they have done a lot of reading and have made some discoveries that they would like to share in a meaningful way. An article or two isn't going to cut it. Neither is a video or a meme. So they put a lot of time into writing a book. But readers are an important part of the conversation. Some people don't read because they think it is isolating and they would rather be with people. But that is an inaccurate understanding of the process. When you read a book, you are engaging with a person—the author. And the intent of the author isn't for you to shut the book and move on with your life, as if this were just a private affair. "Reading a book is a kind of conversation," and the reader now has a duty to reciprocate.[2] There are all kinds of ways to engage in the conversation, the easiest being just to talk about these ideas with others or to share the book. But my next point takes it one step further.

Read books to develop critical skills of discernment. Joining the conversation should be more than regurgitating ideas. Adler and Van Doren have some great advice regarding our teachability:

> A person is wrongly thought to be teachable if he is passive and pliable. On the contrary, teachability is an extremely active virtue. No one is really teachable who does not freely exercise his power of independent judgment. He can be trained, perhaps, but not taught. *The most teachable reader is, therefore, the most critical.*[3]

This is an art that is lacking in the church. Animals can be trained; people ask questions, look for propositions and points of persuasion, and interact with ideas. Our lack of intelligent reading has prevented us from developing these critical skills.

Read books in order to learn. Adler and Van Doren hold "that knowledge can be communicated and that discussion can result in learning."[4] If we believe that every claim a person makes is merely an opinion that is equal to all other opinions, then there

2. Ibid., 137.
3. Ibid., 140 (emphasis in original).
4. Ibid., 149.

really isn't much of a reason to read books. But if we believe that truth has content and that we can appeal to that through reason and logic, then we should be truth-seekers. And this gives us a purpose for reading—to learn! An author with a likable personality is certainly a bonus, but I read in order to learn something from a book, and that helps me to finish the book.

Good books last longer than blog posts, which fade into cyberspace, hoping that a Google search will bring them to light again one day. And they seek a higher purpose in shaping a reader. Read for discovery and understanding, not just to gather information. Read to develop your critical-thinking skills. Be teachable and then teach others. Read books!

Before You Read the Book

Part of becoming a good reader is learning what to do before you make the commitment to read. Reading a book is like going on a date. Many people are just plain overwhelmed when it comes to reading good books. While they may have an inclination to learn, they so often don't persevere in engaging with a book, much less with the many other books they could continue to read afterwards. I see this especially when it comes to reading books on theology. But reading is an active exercise. You wouldn't want to take out a prospective good date and then be a bore all evening, would you? And you need to ask the right person out to the right occasion. In other words, you need to be good at sizing up a book.

Let's say that you want to approach a guy and ask him out. If all you've seen him in is a suit and tie, you most likely shouldn't ask him to be your partner in the Tough Mudder competition when it comes to town—at least not until you get to know him better.

Likewise, when you first meet your new book, you need to make some observations and develop a reading strategy. We all tend to take a look at the cover and maybe at the endorsements on the back. Most of us will do a quick scan of the table of contents to get a better idea of what we are getting into. But here are some additional tips that can help you not to fall asleep on your date—I mean, book—and be more engaging.

Be Realistic

Go ahead and put some time goals on your date. How many pages are in the book? This is simple math. Let's say that your book is one hundred eighty pages long. If you are finding it hard at first to carve out good reading time (or to concentrate for long periods of time), commit to ten pages a day. You will be finished with your book in a little over two weeks—not too shabby! It's not all that much of a sacrifice to give twenty minutes of your time for a mere eighteen days. With a longer book, do the same thing. You can stick to your ten pages and spend a month or so on it, or you can bump it up to twenty pages or more per day.

When you ask someone on a date, you are setting aside time for him. You don't let a bunch of silly distractions end your time together. That is, unless the date really stinks. Then you should have an exit plan. It's okay to walk out on a book if it is just not meeting your expectations. But that leads to the next point.

Come with a Clear Expectation

What is it that you would like to get out of this book? Are you trying to grow in an area in which you already have some knowledge? Are you trying to learn about something completely new? You will be able to get an idea from the introduction whether your expectations are realistically going to be met. What do you suspect that the author is going to say?

Are you coming into the book with an open mind, or do you think you are going to be disagreeing with the material? Either way, how would it be enriching for you to read this book? Remember, when you are spending time with a book, you are spending time with an author. These expectations will help to guide your time with a book.

Aim a Bit Out of Your League

I know, I just told you to be realistic; but people somehow marry up all the time. And if you want to grow as a reader, you must read *above* your reading level. While comprehension is important, so is learning. Remember, just because something is difficult, it shouldn't stop us. Instead of quitting when we don't immediately understand, we should actively engage in order to grow in our understanding. There are methods we can employ to grow in our comprehension. We need to be challenged to grow, not coddled and encouraged to stay where we are. I'd prefer that my daughter read a book she doesn't completely understand and work hard for a B grade than get an A by reading something that is easy for her. Sure, sometimes it's okay and even good to read material that comes easily, but to grow in understanding we must read something challenging.

And the same principle goes for adults. We know that people who are smarter than us, kinder than us, or more athletic than us can give us that extra push we need to grow. But for some reason we don't always look at books that way. A book may be on a topic that we are really interested in, and we may even be excited about the particular author. But as soon as we stumble over a concept in it, we conclude that the book just isn't for us. But maybe this book is *exactly* for us— for that very reason! It would be better to think, *This book is over my head, and maybe I could really grow in my understanding from reading it.*

But this requires an active engagement from the reader. Adler and Van Doren compare the reader to the catcher in a baseball game. Just because the catcher receives the pitch, it doesn't mean that his job is inactive. Adler and Van Doren's whole book equips the reader to read actively. Unfortunately, it's over four hundred pages of reading about reading. Reading it is time well spent, but I'll summarize some of their ideas for you.

The authors discuss different levels of reading. In their chapter on inspectional reading, they explain that sometimes our expectations are set too high when we pick up a difficult book, and we mistakenly give up when we realize that our expectations won't be met. When you are up against a book that is "over your head," they recommend doing a superficial reading of the entire book first. You may not get full comprehension the first time through. But that doesn't mean that you cannot grow in your understanding. So their rule is, *"In tackling a difficult book for the first time, read it through without ever stopping to look up or ponder the things you do not understand right away."*[5]

Just keep reading. Read through the parts that you may not grasp, and eventually you will find some balls that you can catch. Adler and Van Doren encourage you to concentrate on those sections that you do understand.

Keep on in this way. Read the book through, undeterred and undismayed by the paragraphs, footnotes, comments, and references that escape you. If you let yourself get stalled, if you allow yourself to be tripped up by any one of these stumbling blocks, you are lost. In most cases, you will not be able to puzzle the thing out by sticking to it. You will have a much

5. Ibid., 36 (emphasis in original).

better chance of understanding it on a second reading, but that requires you to have read the book *through* at least once.[6]

What? A second time? Yes! Read the stinking book again, and the understanding that you gained in the first run through will help you with your second date, which will hopefully be less superficial. But Adler and Van Doren promise that even the superficial reading alone can be enlightening. "And even if you never go back, understanding half of a really tough book is much better than not understanding it at all, which will be the case if you allow yourself to be stopped by the first difficult passage you come to."[7]

This is the same thing that fitness trainers tell you about surviving one of their workouts for the first time. You may not complete the prescribed duration of each exercise. You might look like a wimp and take too many water breaks. Your push-ups may be laughable at first. Heck, you might even puke. But, if you persevere to the end, you have taken a great step in increasing your fitness level. Your body is beginning to change. Sometimes it hurts. Get over it. You'll do better the next time—and the one after that.

Don't settle for a book that doesn't challenge you. If you want to grow, you need to read up.

How to Be an Engaging Reader

Okay, good; you have prepared for your date. You've sized up your book, you've moved past the intimidation stage, and now you're pretty impressed to be dating out of your league. Now we can move on to getting the most out of your date.

6. Ibid., 36–37 (emphasis in original).
7. Ibid., 37.

And here is where it would get weird if you were actually on a date. It would probably raise some red flags if you showed up with a notebook with questions that you want answered and space to take notes, but it could be really helpful if your date is a book. Active readers have different tools that they may prefer to have handy. I personally love to pick out a Crayola Twistable colored pencil for underlining and marking in my book, as well as a pack of Post-it Flags, which I affectionately call tabbies, to mark pages that I may want to return to later. You may or may not want to have an actual notebook handy, but it could be a helpful tool for forming good habits and growing as a reader. Here are some questions that you will want to ask and answer as you read, as well as some ways that you can further communicate what you are learning.

What Can I Learn from This Book?

This one goes back to our expectations before we read. Write down what questions you hope to have answered before you begin reading. And I know that I said it may be a strange thing to do on an actual date, but my friend Dana does something similar to this before our get-togethers, and I really appreciate it. We don't get to see each other as often as we'd like, so Dana keeps a "cheat sheet" going on a piece of paper that she keeps in a kitchen drawer. She updates it with quick scribbles of all the things she wants to share with me, topics she wants to discuss, and questions she may want to ask during our short time together. Preparing the cheat sheet beforehand ensures that she won't forget all that she was hoping to achieve in our time together. It keeps us absorbed in meaningful conversation (well, it's not all meaningful; some of it is just plain fun) when we do have the opportunity to hang out.

So while you are reading, keep these questions in mind. You can go back and write in your notebook how those questions are answered—or if they are answered at all. Most of the time, when I'm reading a good book, it leads me to ask new questions that I never thought of before picking it up. Write down your new questions and think about where you may look for answers. One of the best treasure troves is the footnotes of the book you are reading. Authors pluck flowers out of books that will hopefully lead you to the garden they came from![8] And you know what they say when you can't find a book that directly addresses something you want to learn more about—it's time for you to research and write that book!

What Do the Author's Terms Mean?

We often encounter new vocabulary when we read a book. We can obviously look up definitions, and we frequently catch on to a word's meaning by the context in which it is used. But sometimes it's trickier to discern the intended meaning when an author is using a word that we are familiar with, but with a meaning that is different from the one we are used to. This is something we should look out for, because it can be misleading. An author may say something like "It's not loving to be intolerant." That sounds good on the surface, but what does he mean by "loving" and what does he mean by "tolerant"? Does "tolerant" mean to accept all behaviors and beliefs as equal, or does it mean being capable of treating someone with kindness and human dignity despite not accepting that person's belief to be true or his behavior to be godly? If the author means the former, I disagree with his statement. It's not loving to be enabling.

We will put this into practice in the next chapter, because

8. See Hannah More, *Collected Works* (London: Harrison and Sons, 1853), 3:120, quoted in Karen Swallow Prior, *Fierce Convictions: The Extraordinary Life of Hannah More; Poet, Reformer, Abolitionist* (Nashville: Nelson Books, 2014), 23.

this is where a reader needs to be sharp. Many people with good intentions accept bad theology because they are not discerning the author's use of certain terms. There are all kinds of words in the Christian vocabulary that get misused to promote un-Christian ideas. So we need to know what authors really mean by the words they use.

Your notebook can come in handy for this. You could have a page for new vocabulary that you are just being introduced to, including these terms' definitions, and you could have a page (or more!) of terms that the author is using that stray from their original meaning. You might be surprised to see words like *repentance, salvation, Trinity,* and *justice* being distorted in "Christian" books.

One of my biggest pet peeves is the use of the word *nice.* Is niceness a Christian virtue? You would think so, according to many books and blogs—especially those directed toward women. But what is niceness, really? It is not the same as kindness. In fact, niceness can be an enemy of the truth. Since the truth is frequently offensive, we try to dip it in a "nice" makeover before we handle it. And at that point, the truth can be unrecognizable. Niceness is the Eddie Haskell of evangelicalism. It's manipulating, but not really loving—manners without truth. Have we become more concerned with politeness than we are with truth? We all are at times. We think that the opposite of *nice* is *mean.* This is not so. Being *nice* is people pleasing, and we like to be popular, don't we? But we need to remember what kind of theologians we are. We are not theologians of our own glory; we are theologians of the cross. Sure, we should be kindhearted. But don't confuse over-groomed caricatures who bird-dog approval with someone who has a kind heart. I catch myself all the time telling my kids that they should be nice. It's a term I need to look out for, even in my own heart!

What Kind of Conversation Do You Find Yourself Having with the Author?

The best readers are active readers. Don't just sit down and expect to absorb a bunch of information. Have an imaginary dialogue going on in your head while reading. Let yourself wonder where the author is going with a particular section. Is he setting you up for something else? Be discerning as you read. Just because your date bought you dinner doesn't mean he can come in for coffee!

And remember that you aren't reading as a blank slate. How does this particular book connect with other things you have read? In particular, how does it measure up to Scripture? Read synoptically. This is a term that Adler and Van Doren use to describe advanced readers who make connections between the different books that they read. Develop some of your own insights as the author is sharing his own. Ask questions. Write them down. The author may address them on the next page, in the next chapter, in a footnote, or not at all. That's why it's good to write a note in your notebook, mark up the page, or stick a tabby on it for later.[9]

This is another reason why I like to use a colored pencil. My daughter did a science fair project on whether things written in colored ink help you to remember better. Red and purple seemed to be two colors that made a positive difference in memory retention.[10] It may or may not help me to remember notable parts of the book better, but it does make it a lot easier to find where I've marked up a book when I'm flipping through it. And it doesn't rub off on my hands like an ordinary pencil does.

9. Remember, this author does not use the word *tabby* according to its original definitions.
10. This is a bit of a rabbit trail, but one that you may want to underline with a red pencil to recall.

You see, we are having a conversation right now about colors, memory, and preferences in tools for marking a book! I've just synoptically connected my daughter's science fair project with Adler and Van Doran's stages in reading.

In this conversation with the author, consider your own arguments on the topic. I am not using the word *argument* as a negative term here; I am referring to our own reasoning and quest for a logical conclusion, whether we agree with the author or not. It's an insult to the author if you finish a book with a nice comment that means absolutely nothing ("Gee, Mrs. Cleaver, I do believe that dinner was swell") and proves that you didn't engage with the material at all. What is the author affirming, denying, insinuating, or neglecting? What assumptions is she making? How are you reacting to the key sentences in your book? Adler and Van Doren point out that there are going to be some sentences that you are likely to stumble over. Those are some of the most important sentences for you to slow down and take a closer look at. The sentences that demand some effort from you to unpack usually contain the important ideas that the author is trying to communicate. Most of the book will probably be spent attempting to explain, support, unpack, and argue those ideas.[11]

Find Ways to Talk about Your Date

One of the best ways to better comprehend what you're reading, retain the information, and personalize the material is to recognize how your reading relates to other conversations you are having. Take your book for a test drive. Let her meet your friends—or your mom, if she's really special. What we read shapes us. Be aware of how your book is affecting your thinking. Maybe the book is written poorly or doesn't shed any

11. See Adler and Van Doren, *How to Read a Book*, 121.

new light. That is okay too, because recognizing this is a sign of discernment. You don't continue to take out a bad date, and you wouldn't want to recommend a bad book to others. But know why it is bad. And if it wasn't necessarily a bad book, but maybe just not a book for you, someone else may benefit from your sharing it with him.

I like to host informal get-togethers with some of my friends and family just to talk about the books we are reading. I call it a book review night. It keeps us accountable for reading, and it helps us to share the ideas and critiques of our books. This is a great way to sharpen our reading skills. Most of the reviews are casual and unwritten, and we cut each other off with added reflections and questions. My "cheat sheet" friend Dana likes to add an artistic flair to her reviews, which is always enlightening and entertaining. These get-togethers have helped us to learn from one another's reading and to discover books that we may not have encountered elsewhere.

Consider Writing a Review

Although you wouldn't want to kiss and tell with a date, books are meant to be publicized, discussed, and even dissected a little. Think about writing a review. You may not be a blogger, but you can still get in on the discussion and inform other readers by leaving a review on a website like Amazon or Goodreads. This not only helps prospective readers but also helps you to articulate your thoughts and even bring up some of those questions that you had. But, as with a date, remember that there is a person behind the book. You wouldn't want to write anything in a review that you wouldn't feel is appropriate to share with the author himself.

Writing out reviews, or even a reading reflection, has helped me to become a better reader. When you are writing a review, it is essential to understand the author's argument and to represent it accurately. This practice has helped to improve my ability to know what I'm looking for in a book. You can use the questions in this chapter to guide you in writing a thoughtful review, rather than just a summary of the book. Reviews can be helpful to the author in drawing attention to his book and also in letting him know how it is being received.[12]

Is the Author Persuasive?

This is a question that usually needs to be answered in a review in one way or another, and it's one that every reader should have on her mind. It may be helpful to track the author's reasons, arguments, and supporting material in your notebook or by markings within the book. Are you convinced? Or maybe you find that the author makes some very good points, and yet you can't follow the whole line of reasoning. Such books are often beneficial to me, because even though I may disagree with some of the main conclusions, my perspective has been changed or some doors may have opened to lead me to discover truths I didn't know before. We can certainly learn from those whom we disagree with, and they usually help us to sharpen our own stance.

Maybe the author is good at pinpointing problems but not very good at offering solutions. That's one reason I wanted to write this chapter and the next. I can make a case that God loves all the women in his church and therefore calls us all to be theologically competent, but am I offering up suggestions on how we can work toward that goal? I can make the

---

12. I do detest the star rating system, though. Interacting directly with the ideas and arguments in a book is one thing. The rating system does not reflect the nuances of that very well, or the different standards that readers will employ. And yet, as an author, I depend on people to leave reviews on these popular sites. Most books are discussed and sold online these days, and that makes marketing a mixed cyber bag. So I go back and forth with the rating system and am generous with books that teach healthy theology.

case that bad doctrine is sneaking into the church through the back door of women's ministries, but am I offering any helpful teaching to equip women to evaluate books that are aimed at them? It isn't easy to decide whether a book is persuasive. I love some books that are persuasive in some areas and not so much in others.

Most books don't answer all my questions. Maybe it's because I have a lot of questions. But, when our questions aren't all answered for us, we are challenged to do some research of our own to get our questions answered. Isn't the Bible kind of like that? God is inexhaustible, and we will always be learning about him and his work. We will always have questions, but we should seek him through his Word for the answers. Do the solutions that are offered in your book square up with God's Word? Where may the author have fallen short? Or where are you unsure about that, and what can you do about it?

I have given you a few ideas to keep you engaged. What helps you to improve as a reader? Do you set reading goals for the year? Do you have something that you would like to learn more about but haven't had the nerve to ask out yet? What keeps you reading, and what keeps you from reading well? Let's put some of these tips into practice in the next chapter. I also want to address a question that you've probably been wondering about.

Questions for Reflection and Discussion

1. When are you most tempted to preserve your own kingdom rather than persevering in God's? What can you implement in order to build competence in God's Word, strengthen your resolve, and exercise proper discernment?
2. In what areas do you think you need the most growth in discernment?

3. Why did you decide to read this book? What expectations did you have before reading it?

4. Do you consider yourself a reader? What books have you read in the last six months? How many of them have challenged you because they were above your theological or literary reading level?

5. Has this book been what you originally expected? In what ways has or hasn't it been what you expected? Has it been enriching? Has one chapter stood out more than others so far? Why?

6. Let's apply my active reading questions to this book. In the introduction, I asked you what you hoped to learn from this book. How's that going? Has *No Little Women* raised any new questions for you since then?

7. Have you encountered any new vocabulary while reading *No Little Women*? If so, what? What are some key terms I have used in this book thus far? Have I used any of them differently from how you would define them?

8. What kind of conversation do you find yourself having with me? How has my book connected with other things you have read? How does it measure up with Scripture? What am I affirming, denying, insinuating, neglecting, or assuming so far? How does that compare with your own arguments? What are some key sentences in this book? Which ones have you stumbled over?

9. Have you been participating in any lively conversations as a result of reading this book? Has *No Little Women* gone on any test drives? If you've answered these questions, you've practically written a review already!

10. Has this book been persuasive? Have any of your perspectives been challenged? Are my solutions in line with Scripture?

11. What questions do you still want to have answered?

HONING AND TESTING OUR DISCERNMENT SKILLS

All the exhortations in this book for us to be competent women and all my warnings against false teaching naturally give rise to questions about how to know when someone has crossed the theological line. How exactly does this discernment thing work? We don't want to be inviting in bad teaching, and yet aren't there many different theological positions within orthodox Christianity? Should we divide over every little thing? Aren't we striving for unity?

Of course we are! But what is it that unites us? We have a beautiful prayer recorded in Scripture, offered by Jesus for the unity of his church (see John 17:11). In it, he prays for his disciples, "Sanctify them in the truth; your word is truth" (John 17:17). To sanctify means to set apart. So we see that Christ's disciples were to be set apart by his word. In addition, he prays for all those who believe in him through the word that his disciples will teach, as he later commissions them to do (see Matt. 28:18–20). We can be united only by the truth; anything else is superficial. God's Word is truth!

And yet there is a setting apart, as truth needs to be separated from lies and error.

But isn't love the most important thing? Even Jesus answered the Pharisee's question regarding which is the greatest commandment by speaking about love:

> You shall love the Lord your God with all your heart and with all your soul and with all your mind. This is the great and first commandment. And a second is like it: You shall love your neighbor as yourself. (Matt. 22:37–39)

Here he is recalling the Shema, Israel's confession found in Deuteronomy 6:4–5, which begins with "Hear, O Israel: The LORD our God, the LORD is one" (v. 4) and then follows with this statement that Jesus echoes. So yes, love is of extreme importance—not only with our hearts and souls, but with our minds as well.

Whom do you love? The issue is that we have no problem setting our affections on many things and many people. But here we see that we need to love the Lord our God, who is one. So we need to make sure that the God we are learning about in any church, Christian book, radio program, conference, or conversation, is the Lord God—the true God whom we learn about in *his* Word. This is of utmost importance! And it is a major theme taught by the apostles. Paul exhorts Timothy to make sure that healthy doctrine is upheld "in accordance with the gospel of the glory of the blessed God with which I have been entrusted" (1 Tim. 1:11). And this begins with knowing the Lord. He teaches the Corinthian church the foolishness of tolerating anyone who "comes and proclaims another Jesus than the one we proclaimed, or if you receive a different spirit from the one you received, or if you accept a different gospel from the one you accepted" (2 Cor. 11:4).

It would be utter foolishness, damning foolishness, to place our love on a different God than the one his Word teaches about and on a different way of salvation. We call that heresy, because it is against what the church has faithfully confessed and taught from Scripture. So, while there are many areas in which Christians will have acceptable theological differences, there are important lines of orthodoxy that must be established. And even for the acceptable differences, we always care about the truth.

Essential Questions to Ask about Theology

There are four big things that we especially need to look for in the views of the authors we read. An author may not be using these precise terms, but her book is going to have some underlying teaching about God's Word, who man is, who God is, and what he has done. We look for this in what the author says, but what she doesn't say can be just as revealing. And this is worth a section in your notebook.

What Does the Author Say about God's Word?

We must begin by knowing God's Word and how Scripture is distinguished from other books. Many books can teach us about and from the Scriptures, but we are responsible to know God's Word and to discern whether what people say is in line with its teachings (see Acts 17:11). We can trust that God's Word is true because God is our source of goodness and truth. But the Bible isn't merely a large book that we can compare all other teachings to. It is the inspired Word of God, meaning that it is God-breathed (see 2 Tim. 3:16). We are not to treat it as words from wise men that we can go to for guidance in life. No, that passage from 2 Timothy is clear that Scripture is

God's Word to his people. It is not just one teaching among others but is direct revelation from our Creator that supplies us with everything we need to live a life of faith and obedience. And God's Word is different from all other words. It is accompanied by his Spirit, which makes it "living and active, . . . discerning the thoughts and intentions of the heart" (Heb. 4:12). Therefore, God's Word is our absolute authority, over even a pastor, elder, husband, or author.

Now, most books aren't going to open with a statement of faith telling you what the author's stance is on God's Word and other essential doctrines. You are going to have to look for how the author uses God's Word and discusses it. The author may say orthodox things about God's Word but then reveal through his handling of it that he in fact believes something different about it. Do the doctrines he is teaching come from Scripture? Is he being faithful in his use of Scripture passages, considering their context and the primary meaning of the text? Or does he seem to be playing fast and loose with it, bending it to fit his own agenda? Reading with discernment means that we need to be good students of the Word. Space doesn't allow me to go through the whole doctrine of the Word of God and hermeneutics, but these are important for a Christian to learn. The more mature you are in the Word, the easier you will notice when an author is using a "yeah, but" argument, downplaying its authority, twisting its meaning, or downright teaching against it.[1]

What Does the Author Say about Who Man Is?

Scripture is clear that, without God, man is totally depraved—that is, unable to do good and naturally inclined to

---

1. Tim Challies, *The Discipline of Spiritual Discernment* (Wheaton, IL: Crossway, 2007), is a helpful book that teaches how to develop discernment skills.

sin.[2] Before the fall of Adam, man was able to do good based on his own righteousness. After the fall, all of our faculties are tainted by sin, and we cannot do good apart from faith (see Rom. 8:7–8; 14:23). We are utterly dependent on the righteousness of Jesus Christ and on his payment for our sin on the cross in order to live an eternal life of holiness with him. Man cannot redeem himself. We are not self-improvers. We are not basically good, so that with a little help and a better environment we can reform. We are utterly lost without Christ. We don't need a sidekick; we need a Savior. And we don't need to get better; we need to be new creations (see Eph. 2:1–10).

We are not God. As obvious as that may sound, the teaching in many books by Christian authors insinuates that we are. Books that promote being better people by following five steps, or some other formula for a successful life now, often set up some sort of ladder for us to climb for self-actualization. That kind of teaching will only leave us in despair. God has to condescend to us; we cannot rise to him. We need to understand that believers and unbelievers have different relationships to the law. The law is certainly good and necessary in the Christian life, but without Christ we cannot follow it; it only condemns us. United to Christ, we are friends with the law again, as it points us to the One who fulfills it and directs us in our sanctification. But we can easily get caught up in doing better to please God and can leave Christ completely out of the picture, or at least give him a secondary role to ours. Christians are people of the gospel. This good news is something outside of ourselves. We don't discover it by navel gazing. Rather, it is a powerful message that we need to hear. We are sinners who are saved by faith alone, not by faith plus works (although

2. See, for example, 2 Chron. 6:36; Ps. 143:2; Isa. 53:6; Luke 18:19; Rom. 3:9–12, 23; 14:23; Eph. 2:3; 1 John 1:8–10.

our faith results in good works). This is a gift received by grace alone, not earned by our merit or good will. Our faith is in Christ alone, not because we said a prayer and can take it from there, but because our justification is completely in him and because our power to live a holy life and our future glorification are based on our union with him. Because of this, God alone gets the glory. Amen!

What Does the Author Say about God?

There are many books labeled Christian that do not have an orthodox teaching about God. This is not a trivial doctrine, but rather a critical confession of our faith. What is God? The Shorter Catechism tells us, "God is a Spirit, infinite, eternal, and unchangeable, in his being, wisdom, power, holiness, justice, goodness, and truth."[3] If you follow the link provided in my footnote, you will find many Scripture references and resources. You see, God wants us to know who he is. And he cares that we get it right. This is our honor and for our good. Every Christian would do well to study the attributes of God. Maybe this encouragement to study sounds too academic. Do we really have to study God in order to have a relationship with him? I use the word *study* because it does require purposeful effort on our part—every relationship does. But the blessings that come out of such a study reveal that it is a delight to the soul and a gift that we never want to divert our eyes from again. And so it is going to bother us when we read authors who downplay his holiness, question his goodness, and subvert his truth.

And, along with this, we need to keep an eye on how an author portrays the Trinity. So many troubling teachings flow

3. "Westminster Shorter Catechism, Question 4," available online at Westminster Shorter Catechism Project, last modified July 30, 2016, http://www.shorter catechism.com/resources/wsc/wsc_004.html.

from a wrong view of the Father, the Son, and the Holy Spirit. It is important for us to learn what God has communicated about himself: that he is one being, one Godhead, in three "persons"—namely the Father, the Son, and the Holy Spirit. The Lord God is one. The Father is God, the Son is God, and the Holy Spirit is God. They are not three separate beings. And yet the Father is not the Son, the Holy Spirit is not the Father, the Son is not the Father, and so on. Furthermore, the second person of the Trinity took human flesh in the incarnation, so that Jesus is fully God and fully man. The Council of Nicaea gathered in 325 to articulate the Bible's teaching on the Trinity and combat heresy.

The Trinity is an essential doctrine, meaning that it is a necessary belief in the Christian faith. The full divinity and full humanity of the Son is also an essential doctrine. After Jesus reiterated the greatest commandment, to love God with all our heart, mind, and soul, he asked the Pharisees whose son the Christ is. They answered according to Scripture that Christ is the son of David. But Jesus pressed further by quoting from God's Word in Psalm 110: "The Lord said to my Lord, 'Sit at my right hand, until I put your enemies under your feet'" (Matt. 22:44; cf. Ps. 110:1). He questioned the Pharisees about how David could call his son "Lord." If he is David's son, how can he also be his Lord? That shut the Pharisees up, for they had no answer. But their answer was standing right in front of them! Jesus, who descended from the line of David, is also the Son of God! David was privy to an intra-Trinitarian conversation, revealed to him by the Spirit of God, of the Father talking to the Son regarding the covenant they had made to redeem a people for himself. The Pharisees refused to see who Christ really was. If an author is not in line with what God says about himself, then you should have serious doubts about what she is teaching you.

What Does the Author Say about What God Has Done and Is Doing?

Every person operates from some sort of worldview regarding creation, fall, redemption, and restoration. It may be helpful to write these categories down in your notebook and fill in how the author engages with these issues in her writing. Usually you are not so lucky as to have the title give it away, but does *Your Best Life Now*[4] align with the gospel? Is the good news simply that we will have our best lives on this side of the resurrection? Are we theologians of glory or theologians of the cross? The gospel reveals that, although as sinners we have offended the holy God, our Creator, and deserve having his wrath poured out on us in order for justice to prevail, he has set his love on us and sent his very Son, Jesus Christ, to live the life that we could not live and die the death that we deserve. On the cross, Jesus encountered the full wrath of God for the sins of his people, and it was finished. Our sin was imputed to Christ so that his righteousness could be imputed to us. In three days, Jesus rose from the dead and appeared to his disciples as well as to over five hundred people. He ascended to the right hand of the Father, where he is now, to intercede on our behalf as an unremitting advocate for his people (as we see in Psalm 110). And he will return for his bride. We await the final resurrection of the saints, when we will be raised with holy, eternal bodies to reign with him in the new heavens and the new earth.

According to his grace and mercy, the Father gives new eyes to his beloved that allow them to see his glory and our sin, leading us to repentance and faith in Christ as new creations sealed with his Holy Spirit. By this faith, we are declared justified and are finally able to do truly good works, which are

4. Joel Osteen, *Your Best Life Now: 7 Steps to Living at Your Full Potential* (New York: FaithWords, 2014).

pleasing to him, in dependence on his Spirit. Christ blesses our efforts as we strive to live a life of faith and obedience, and in this process he is transforming us into his own likeness. We fall a lot. We continue to fight sin to its death. But we fight. We repent. We hate sin. We endure hardships and trials in this life, which is still affected by the curse of sin from the fall. But it is our privilege now to partner with Christ in our sufferings as we look to him for the strength to persevere and run for the great reward, which is eternal life with him. Then there will be no more tears and no more sin. To God be the glory!

How does the author's message line up with the glorious news of the gospel? In Galatians 1:6–9, Paul warns the church not to believe any other gospel:

> I am astonished that you are so quickly deserting him who called you in the grace of Christ and are turning to a different gospel—not that there is another one, but there are some who trouble you and want to distort the gospel of Christ. But even if we or an angel from heaven should preach to you a gospel contrary to the one we preached to you, let him be accursed.

Those are very strong words. But they are loving words! It isn't loving to accept any teaching in the church that is damning to our souls. What teaching is Paul referring to? He is combating the false teaching of the Judaizers here. Interestingly, their teaching has a lot in common with orthodox Christianity. We might think that the differences aren't that big of a deal:

> They believed in one God, who exists eternally in three Persons: the Father, Son, and Holy Spirit. They believed in the deity and humanity of Christ. They believed that He was Israel's Messiah in fulfillment of the Old Testament. They

believed in penal substitutionary atonement—that Christ bore the punishment of God's wrath against the sins of His people when He died on the cross, so that they might be free from sin's penalty and power (and one day its presence). They believed that He was buried, and that He rose on the third day. And they believed that repentance and faith in Christ was absolutely necessary for forgiveness of sins and fellowship with God in heaven. That is a *lot* of *really* important doctrine that they got right!

Their one issue boiled down, basically, to whether good works were the *cause* or the *result* of salvation. Was law-keeping the *ground* or merely the *evidence* of saving faith? Are we saved by faith *alone*, or by faith in Christ *plus* our religious observance?[5]

Maybe we would think that the differences are minor, but Paul's language will not allow that. The message of the gospel is "the power of God for salvation to everyone who believes" (Rom. 1:16). Why would we steer away from *the* good news?

Putting Our Doctrines through Triage

Albert Mohler wrote a helpful article that many Christians refer to when it comes to our disagreements over doctrine.[6] In it, he uses the illustration of the triage process in the emergency room of a hospital to help us to prioritize the danger levels of doctrinal differences. This illustration really helps us to get a better understanding of what we are dealing with. Everyone

5. Mike Riccardi, "Bad Doctrine vs. Heresy: An Exercise in Theological Triage," *The Cripplegate* (blog), November 19, 2015, http://thecripplegate.com/bad-doctrine -vs-heresy-an-exercise-in-theological-triage/.

6. See Albert Mohler, "A Call for Theological Triage and Christian Maturity," AlbertMohler.com, July 12, 2005, http://www.albertmohler.com/2005/07/12/a -call-for-theological-triage-and-christian-maturity/.

who needs emergency medical attention is unhealthy. Have you ever been in an ER? It's uncomfortable, to say the least. There are suffering faces all around and family members in panic. The room is full of fear, anxiety, sorrow, and desperation. And then there are the germs! It's not a place that you want to hang around in. And yet not every illness and injury is equal. Medical professionals have to assess the threat level as they prioritize which patients the doctors will see first. So someone who is having a heart attack, or a child who has been hit by a car, is going to get priority over a really bad sinus infection or migraine. The hospital staff is trained to ask specific questions and make pertinent observations to decide which patients need immediate attention and which conditions can endure the wait. These aren't always easy decisions to make. Some are clearer than others, and everyone is going to be seen by a doctor, but it is a helpful way to persevere through the tasks at hand. Without this method, the chaos of emergency medical problems would be overwhelming.

Likewise, faced with parachurch ministries, information on the Internet, Christian books, celebrity pastors, and podcasts, we may be overwhelmed as we try to discern which doctrines need to be protected and which ones may not need immediate surgery. All theological error is unhealthy, for sure. But the essentials, such as the authority of Scripture, the Trinity, the deity and humanity of Christ, and justification by faith, are what Mohler calls "first-order" doctrines that are necessary for a Christian to believe. Any teachings that contradict first-order doctrines are heretical.

Mohler then distinguishes two more levels of theological triage. "Second-order" doctrines, also called "secondary" doctrines, are those that are so important that they will affect our corporate worship but do not stop us from counting one another as brothers and sisters in Christ. And, as a result, we have different denominations within Christianity. Baptism is a good example of this. Presbyterians and Baptists are not both right on the meaning and mode of baptism. Both strongly believe that their understanding of baptism is closest to God's Word. And yet, both believe the important matter that all communicant members in God's household need to be baptized. We also both believe that the act of baptism does not create new life but is rather a sign and a seal of the work of Christ in his death and resurrection. So we agree on the importance of the sacrament, but our differences are important enough to cause us to worship separately. Teaching on church government can also be a second-order doctrine. Mohler also regards the ordination or non-ordination of women as a second-order doctrine.

He then adds a "third-order" category of doctrine for sorting in theological triage. This category is for differences that are real and important, but not ones that would necessarily keep us from worshipping together in the same congregation. He uses the example that Christians can maintain close fellowship while still having differences in belief about the details of Christ's return—the doctrine of eschatology, as we call it.

This can be a helpful guide, but we are responsible to know Scripture, to look at the historic confessions of the church in opposition to heresy, and to exercise wisdom and discernment as we read. We need to take theology seriously, but we also need to do our triage with humility. We can't just call someone a heretic because we strongly disagree with her. We need to be careful not to put second- and third-order doctrines in the first-order category. And yet we are to pursue truth and treat all theological error as unhealthy. We may recognize a difference as secondary, but it may still be an important matter that shouldn't be downplayed. After all, we want to grow in our knowledge of the truth, not to become complacent.

And we should strive to sharpen one another in a friendly

manner. This is where denominational boundaries can be helpful. If we are upfront about our theological distinctives, we then have a platform from which to let others know what confessions we align with the most. This way, we aren't being manipulative in our conversations and with our teaching. With proper boundaries set in place, we can acknowledge where we agree and disagree, all with the common goal of sharpening one another according to the Word of God and the working of his Spirit. But this requires a resolve to take theology seriously, take ourselves less seriously, and desire to grow in a meaningful way. Pretending that we are all on the same page and overlooking important differences can only foster a superficial unity that is not based on Christ's Word.

Reading as Triage

Mohler's illustration of theological triage is helpful for us to put into practice while we read. Remember, we are reading for understanding, discovery, growth, and conversation. Reading with an open mind does not mean we will accept anything that we read, but rather that we are willing to give anyone a chance for critical engagement. The more engaged we are with Scripture, the better our triage skills will be and the more equipped we'll be to recognize good books. We don't want to be hanging out in the theological emergency room all the time. We want to enjoy healthy theology that leads to a joyful, mature life in Christ. People who read a steady diet of poorly written, bad theology books probably haven't spent time with the good stuff. At least that is my hope. The other possibility is that they have rebelled against the good stuff.

We can be enriched by authors who hold different doctrines from us on secondary issues. And, just as we may need emergency care for cardiac arrest while our liver is perfectly healthy, so there are authors who may have serious theological error in one area of doctrine while having a lot to teach us in another. This is not ideal, of course, because we don't want to be partially healthy. Authors like this require more discernment and maturity from a reader. We need to be astute enough to realize that even those who teach heretical doctrine have some attractive qualities and may even make some observations about us that we need to hear. But that doesn't mean we should accept their heresy or downplay healthy teaching.

While there is a lot of heresy being sold by the Christian book industry, books marketed for and popular with Christian women could often be diagnosed as having autoimmune diseases. Without a thorough inspection, they seem to have some good points and experiences that women can relate to. But the authors tend not to have a sound theological immune system. They don't have doctrinal clarity and maturity. And yet they feel like they have some enthusiasm for the faith and some understanding of women's struggles that they want to share and teach from. Inevitably what happens is that they begin attacking healthy teaching in a subversive kind of way, causing all kinds of inflammation and various chronic conditions that weaken the church. For some reason, they do not react well to attempts to correct them, and they want to continue overactively spreading their messages. There are all kinds of different autoimmune symptoms to look out for now, but there are three dangerous ideas that are commonly found in the best-selling Christian books for women.

Ecumenicalism at the Expense of Doctrine

Look, we can sell more books if we can appeal to more Christians, right? Plus, we want to focus on unity in love, not on dividing over doctrine. To be ecumenical is to reach out to Christians who do not share our denominational distinctives.

This is a worthy ambition! But we find unity in truth. We should never downplay or contradict the teachings of Scripture for the purpose of unity—it doesn't work! Unfortunately, what I am finding is exactly that: an appeal to a wide audience with a superficial unity. The author tends not to go into detail about important teaching on sin, repentance, justice, holiness, and salvation so that no one will be offended. The readers then rely on the author's perception of what is good, the author's version of Jesus, and the author's message of how to live the Christian life. I would rather read from someone who has clear doctrinal distinctives that are different from mine but who is still seeking unity based on a serious reading of God's Word.

Claiming Direct Revelation from God

Many authors will affirm the authority of Scripture and yet attribute the same authority to a subjective message that they feel God is giving them. They say it in different ways. Some say that God lays the message on their heart. Some say that they hear a small whisper. Some talk more like they have had a vision. But many of these authors are claiming to teach from a message that God has specifically given to them outside of Scripture. And many will present this as if it would be disobedient to God if they did not follow it. It is authoritative. Well, I'd have to agree that if God is talking, it is absolutely authoritative! But Scripture teaches us that God has spoken to us in these last days by his Son and that we now have God's complete Word. We do not need any extra words from him. We do need to intimately know the Word he has given us. We need to study it so that we not only know his precepts but also know his character behind them. And he will give us wisdom to make personal decisions.

Sure, it would be much easier if I could hear a voice from God that said, "Aimee, do not take that job!" But that is not the way that God has ordained for us to grow in faith. While he does lead us by his Spirit, we do not hear direct revelation. And it is only after the fact that I can look back and confirm that, yes, that was the work of the Spirit that prompted me in that direction. One thing I can know for sure is that the Spirit never operates apart from his Word. It is tempting to use the excuse that God is telling us to do something if we don't want to be challenged on a decision we are making or a teaching we are sharing. But he has made it clear that

> All Scripture is breathed out by God and profitable for teaching, for reproof, for correction, and for training in righteousness, that the man of God may be complete, equipped for every good work. (2 Tim. 3:16–17)

Don't let an author substitute the authority and sufficiency of Scripture with her own words. Make her do the work of going to God's Word for teaching.

Bad Hermeneutics

Often authors are not skilled in interpreting the meaning of Scripture. The Bible contains many different types of literature, such as historical narrative, poetry, wisdom literature, apocalyptic literature, prophetic literature, and epistles. To read it literally means that we need to read it according to what is called the grammatico-historical method. These are fancy words, but they point to basic reading strategy. We are to look for the writer's original meaning, based on the genre of the literature, the grammar, and the context in which he is speaking. We should do that with everything we read. However, too often authors will read their own meaning into a text—one that fits their own teaching—rather than studying the passage and submitting to the meaning that is in the text. Often an author makes good and valid points while using poor exposition of

Scripture to prove them, and that is a shame. Since there are many verses in Scripture that are difficult to interpret, and since Scripture never contradicts itself, a helpful principle to follow is to go to easier texts in God's Word to help us to interpret a more difficult one. We should be upfront if we are unsure. But we should never play fast and loose with God's Word.

So these are some common symptoms of books on the best-seller list that reveal autoimmune disease in popular Christian literature. Nobody wants that! But the question is, how good are you at triage?

Presenting the Symptoms

In lieu of discussion questions, we'll end this chapter on an even more practical note: with actual examples from popular books available in Christian bookstores that I've put through a little triage. This is just a sampling. It is far better to size up a book in its entirety, but hopefully these excerpts will give you some practice to get started with. Take a look at them and do some more separating and sorting of truth from error. Remember the questions that you should be asking. Remember to examine how an author is using her terms. If you are having trouble with a text, go to Scripture. Write down some questions. Go over the essentials provided in the chapter. Look for answers. Maybe the problem is more what the text doesn't say than what it does say. Some of these examples may be easy, and some may be more difficult.

Just as in triage, unless it's something like a gunshot wound, you are unlikely to make a complete diagnosis with a look at an excerpt. But you will probably be able to get an idea of how to sort the material for further examination later. I have already done some sorting, but the books could be organized differently. I don't share these so that you can stamp a book with a label of condemnation or collect a list of authors as game for heresy hunting. They are here to give a brief sampling of popular "Christian" books, to hone your discernment skills, and maybe to raise a few red flags. Take note of what is true, what is distorted, what is false, and what just doesn't make sense. Maybe what the author is teaching is true, but her exposition of the Scripture text is bad. In cases where these excerpts are part of an exposition of Scripture, I will first provide the Scripture for you. So get out your marking tools and let's get to it.

Bible Expositions

First, let's take a look at some Bible expositions. Open up your Bibles and take a look at the context for the text indicated. What do you think is the main thrust of the text? Look at the author's exposition and application. Do you see anything healthy there? Do you see any problems with it? What level of triage would you put the mishandling of Scripture in? Do you think that these three excerpts are on the same level, or do one or two stand out to you as more damaging?

> **2 Kings 6:1–7:** Now the sons of the prophets said to Elisha, "See, the place where we dwell under your charge is too small for us. Let us go to the Jordan and each of us get there a log, and let us make a place for us to dwell there." And he answered, "Go." Then one of them said, "Be pleased to go with your servants." And he answered, "I will go." So he went with them. And when they came to the Jordan, they cut down trees. But as one was felling a log, his axe head fell into the water, and he cried out, "Alas, my master! It was borrowed." Then the man of God said, "Where did it fall?" When he showed him the place, he cut off a stick and threw it in there and made the iron float. And he said, "Take it up." So he reached out his hand and took it.

Excerpt (a second point of exposition on the text): *The servant was doing something good when he lost his cutting edge.* He was being productive, building a new dwelling for himself and for those others involved in the school of the prophets (v. 2). In fact, if he hadn't been working so hard—if he'd just been sitting around doing nothing—there's little chance the ax would've ever become gradually loosened and ultimately dislodged. This tells me that being engaged in good, even godly, productive things is not an automatic guard against losing your cutting edge. In fact, one of Satan's dirtiest little tactics is to sneak in and steal it while you're square in the middle of investing yourself in worthwhile activities.[7]

∞

Psalm 41:1–2: Blessed is the one who considers the poor! In the day of trouble the LORD delivers him; the LORD protects him and keeps him alive; he is called blessed in the land; you do not give him up to the will of his enemies.

Psalm 34:10: The young lions suffer want and hunger; but those who seek the LORD lack no good thing.

Proverbs 21:13: Whoever closes his ear to the cry of the poor will himself call out and not be answered.

Excerpt: So many money problems can be solved by putting all finances under God's covering and doing what He says to do with them. That means giving when He says to give. When you do, God promises to deliver you, protect

---

7. Priscilla Shirer, *Fervent: A Woman's Battle Plan for Serious, Specific, and Strategic Prayer* (Nashville: B&H, 2015), 32–33 (emphasis in original).

you, bless you, heal you, and keep you alive. When you don't, you will experience the same desolation the poor do.[8]

6∂

Exodus 18:17–23: Moses' father-in-law replied, "What you are doing is not good. You and these people who come to you will only wear yourselves out. The work is too heavy for you; you cannot handle it alone. Listen now to me and I will give you some advice, and may God be with you. You must be the people's representative before God and bring their disputes to him. Teach them the decrees and laws, and show them the way to live and the duties they are to perform. But select capable men from all the people— men who fear God, trustworthy men who hate dishonest gain—and appoint them as officials over thousands, hundreds, fifties and tens. Have them serve as judges for the people at all times, but have them bring every difficult case to you; the simple cases they can decide themselves. That will make your load lighter, because they will share it with you. If you do this and God so commands, you will be able to stand the strain, and all these people will go home satisfied." (NIV)

Excerpt (an introduction to the text): There's an interesting story in the Old Testament where Jethro, Moses' father-in-law, had to step in and help Moses unrush a season of his life.[9]

8. Stormie Omartian, *The Power of a Praying Wife* (Eugene, OR: Harvest House Publishers, 1997), 56.

9. Lysa TerKeurst, *The Best Yes: Making Wise Decisions in the Midst of Endless Demands* (Nashville: Nelson Books, 2014), 183.

Gospel Presentation

Next we have a gospel presentation. This is the only gospel presentation in the entire book, which is a Christian book about making wise choices. Do you see anything wrong with the author's description of the incarnation? Also, do we make Jesus Lord by our "Best Yes" decision-making skills, or is he Lord whether we say yes to that or not? Since this is the only gospel presentation in the book, what important elements is it leaving out?

> **Excerpt:** It is difficult to embrace an intimate relationship with someone we never see. God understood this, so He physically came to earth and took on another name: Jesus. The absolute Best Yes we'll ever give is asking Jesus Christ to be "the LORD God" over our lives. When we receive Him, we receive life everlasting. But this is just the starting place. We must walk with Him daily, using His gift of wisdom with each and every decision.[10]

Meaning of Terms

Let's triage the next section as excerpts that require us to define the author's meaning behind her terms. This first excerpt is also a sort of gospel presentation. There are some terms here that we will recognize, but how are they used? What is the author saying about sin, a term that isn't used? How do we "receive" Christ's "full redemption"? Do we merely "shamelessly receive" forgiveness of our sins, or do we ask for forgiveness? Go through every line and define the terms as the author is using them. And good luck with the last line.

10. Ibid., 112.

Excerpt: But, if we're willing to give up our addiction to shame,

to believe what He's done,

to receive His full redemption

and the forgiveness of all our sins,

and consider ourselves outrageously loved

and valiantly pursued,

we, my friend, are about to run free in the wide-open liberty of audacity.[11]

Here is another excerpt with terms that need to be defined. When we read a familiar term like *repentance*, it's easy to read our own definition into the author's, but is an element missing in the author's definition here? Related to that, is there something else important that we need to be *asking* for? How significant is this to our salvation and sanctification?

Excerpt: So as you begin crafting a strategy for crushing Satan's backdoor assault on your daily freedom and joy, think back again to that helpful guide we've been using:

- *Praise:* Thank Him for completely forgiving you, cleansing you, changing you.
- *Repentance:* See the foolishness of anything that perpetuates old sin patterns, and by His Spirit walk away.
- *Asking:* Ask for freedom, for release, for the ability to deflect lies and embrace truth.
- *Yes:* Because you, by His resurrection power, can now walk in a new way of life.[12]

11. Beth Moore, *Audacious* (Nashville: B&H, 2015), 53.
12. Shirer, *Fervent*, 101 (emphasis in original).

6o

How does this author use the term *love*? How would you say that Scripture uses the term? To whom does the author of this excerpt give authority—the reader or the Word?

Excerpt: For those who count the Bible as sacred, interpretation is not a matter of *whether* to pick and choose, but *how* to pick and choose. We are all selective. We all wrestle with how to interpret and apply the Bible to our lives. We all go to the text looking for something, and we all have a tendency to find it. So the question we have to ask ourselves is this: Are we reading with the prejudice of love or are we reading with the prejudices of judgment and power, self-interest and greed?[13]

6o

How is the author using the term *eucharisteo*? How exactly do we "lean into the ugly"? Does she give an orthodox explanation of the Lord's Supper? Can we transfigure all things with our *eucharisteo*?

Excerpt: Because *eucharisteo* is how Jesus, at the Last Supper, showed us to transfigure all things—take the pain that is given, give thanks for it, and transform it into a joy that fulfills all emptiness. I have glimpsed it: *This, the hard* eucharisteo. The *hard* discipline to lean into the ugly and whisper thanks to transfigure it into beauty.[14]

---

13. Rachel Held Evans, *A Year of Biblical Womanhood* (Nashville: Thomas Nelson, 2012), 296 (emphasis in original).

14. Ann Voskamp, *One Thousand Gifts: A Dare to Live Fully Right Where You Are* (Grand Rapids: Zondervan, 2010), 100.

∿

Here's something else on the doctrine of sin. Is sin its own punishment? What may be truthful or attractive about that statement? What does this statement say about justice, a word not used in the sentence even though that is what is alluded to here? Does Christianity reduce judgment day and Christ's work on the cross to God punishing sin? Why does God have wrath against sin? Whom do we offend the most when we sin—ourselves? Why would God the Father be represented by a woman?

> **Excerpt (spoken by the allegorical representation of the Father God, who is Papa, an African-American woman):**
> I don't need to punish people for sin. Sin is its own punishment, devouring you from the inside. It's not my purpose to punish it; it's my joy to cure it.[15]

Multiple Issues

There is a lot to agree with in this excerpt, and yet I would triage it in a few categories. I see a false dichotomy and bad hermeneutics, as well as downplaying the authority and sufficiency of Scripture. Do we have to make a choice between legalism and obeying a subjective voice that may or may not be from the Spirit? Also, the excerpt is applying teaching from these two verses in Galatians. What does Paul teach as the meaning of following the Spirit in this section of Galatians? How will we know that we are in step with the Spirit, according to Galatians 5:16–26? And if the Spirit does speak, he speaks with the authority of God—so how do we then "blow it" if we are obeying God's command?

---

15. Wm. Paul Young, *The Shack* (Newbury Park, CA: Windblown Media, 2007), 122.

Galatians 5:18: But if you are led by the Spirit, you are not under the law.

Galatians 5:25: If we live by the Spirit, let us also keep in step with the Spirit.

Excerpt: Following the Spirit also takes discernment. Insight. Perception. And, since we are human, that means most of us who take the risk of being led by the Spirit rather than a list of laws will get it wrong sometimes.

We'll probably look foolish sometimes.

Have to say we blew it sometimes.

But I will say this without a single hesitation: I would rather err trying to obey God than play it safe and quench His Spirit. . . .

It takes some audacity to put yourself out there and live by the Spirit. After all, what if you misunderstand? What if you are wrong?[16]

Intimacy with God

Here are some excerpts on our intimacy with God. What about these passages do you think is appealing to the reader? Are they faithful to Scripture? What is troubling about them? What important doctrines might they be contradicting? How can this be dangerous?

Excerpt: This practice of listening to God has increased my intimacy with Him more than any other spiritual discipline, so I want to share some of the messages I have received.[17]

---

16. Moore, *Audacious*, 165.
17. Sarah Young, *Jesus Calling* (Nashville: Thomas Nelson, 2004), xiii.

Excerpt: I want to be in God and God to be in me, to exchange love and blessings and caresses and, like the apostle-pilgrims, my eyes open and I know it is because of this burning of the heart: this moment is a divine interchange. I raise my hand slightly, finger imperceptibly the air before the canvas and this is intercourse disrobed of its connotations, pure and unadulterated: a passing between. . . .

The intercourse of soul with God is the very climax of joy.[18]

Excerpt: Recently God spoke to me about capturing what He and I are calling "Sabbath moments." Like many of yours, my schedule right now is particularly tough, and I see no time in the near future for a number of days off. God spoke to my heart one Saturday morning while I was preparing for Sunday school: "My child, in between more intense rests, I want to teach you to take Sabbath moments." I wasn't certain what He meant. . . .

I got in my car and prayed. I pulled out of the parking garage, fighting the tears. A few blocks later as if on autopilot, I turned my steering wheel straight into the parking lot of the Houston Zoo!

Christ seemed to say, "Let's go play." And that we did. I hadn't been to the zoo in years. I heard about all the improvements, but I never expected the ultimate: Starbucks coffee! . . . Can you imagine watching a baby koala take a nap in a tree on a rare cold day in Houston with a Starbucks

18. Voskamp, *One Thousand Gifts*, 217–18.

grande cappuccino in your hand? Now that's a Sabbath moment! God and I had a blast.[19]

Claims about God's Word

Again, here are some more excerpts that make interesting claims about God's Word. These are even bolder. The first excerpt has an interesting take on the preached Word. Can we ever develop an immunity to sermons? What does that say about the effectiveness of God's Word? Where does the author place authoritative teaching, in God's Word or in man's actions? What is attractive about this? Is there a hint of truth in there that might make you nod your head with her on the importance of action well done? What is the danger in this assertion?

Excerpt: Consequently, I have heard more sermons, talks, messages, and lectures on Christianity than can possibly be impactful. I have spent half my life listening to someone else talk about God.

Because of this history, I've developed something of an immunity to sermons. . . . Teaching by example, radical obedience, justice, mercy, activism, and sacrifice wholly inspires me. I am at that place where "well done" trumps "well said."[20]

$$\mathit{6\!\circ\!\circ}$$

This book was popular among both men and women. These assertions sound clever, but are they true? Has God's voice been reduced to paper? Is authority really in the hands of the intellectuals who claim to hold the power of interpretation?

---

19. Beth Moore, *The Beloved Disciple: Following John to the Heart of Jesus* (Nashville: B&H, 2003), 220. Thanks to Todd Pruitt for bringing this text to my attention.
20. Jen Hatmaker, *7: An Experimental Mutiny against Excess* (Nashville: B&H, 2012), 23.

Do we put God in a box by trusting in Scripture? And think about the irony of an author using the medium of paper in a book to communicate his angst about written communication.

> **Excerpt:** In seminary he had been taught that God had completely stopped any overt communication with moderns, preferring to have them only listen to and follow sacred Scripture, properly interpreted, of course. God's voice had been reduced to paper, and even that paper had to be moderated and deciphered by the proper authorities and intellects. It seemed that direct communication with God was something exclusively for the ancients and uncivilized, while educated Westerners' access to God was mediated and controlled by the intelligentsia. Nobody wanted God in a box, just in a book. Especially an expensive one bound in leather with gilt edges, or was that guilt edges?[21]

Irreconcilable Exhortations

Here is a triage group that gives exhortations that just don't reconcile with Scripture. According to Scripture, what requirements are there for us to have a saving relationship with Jesus Christ? Compare that to the ones given in this first excerpt.

> **Excerpt:** Unlike a human star [celebrity], Jesus can give such individual attention without excluding others. Every single person in the crowd could have their own individual encounter with Him. The only requirements are the *desire* to experience Him and the *belief* that it is possible.[22]

21. Young, *The Shack*, 67–68.
22. Lysa TerKeurst, *Becoming More Than a Good Bible Study Girl* (Grand Rapids: Zondervan, 2009), 152 (emphasis in original).

This author is sharing a monastic practice called seven sacred pauses. Does Scripture ever even insinuate that we need to find our souls? Are we to be taught by something as vague as anointing rhythms that we need to seek out each day? Are we to empty ourselves, creating a white space, in order to gain our souls? What does this even mean?

> **Excerpt:** Each pause has a focus, and like Wiederkehr explains, "Each day we are summoned to be creators of the present moment. Artists know the value of white space. Sometimes what isn't there enables us to see what is. Perhaps you are being called to the spiritual practice of bringing a little of the white space—of *nada*—into your workday. There in that white space you will find your soul waiting for you. Allow the anointing rhythm of the hours to touch and teach you each day."[23]

Where in the world does Scripture require women to be all these things below? And no, that is not what Proverbs 31 says. What does it even mean to be sexually appealing? Who decides whether we are good enough cooks? And what is the good news in this passage?

> **Excerpt:** Even if you are the only one working and your husband stays home to keep the house and tend the kids, you will still be expected to see that the heart of your home is a peaceful sanctuary—a source of contentment,

---

23. Hatmaker, 7, 183, quoting from Macrina Wiederkehr, *Seven Sacred Pauses: Living Mindfully Through the Hours of the Day* (Notre Dame, IN: Sorin Books, 2008), 13.

acceptance, rejuvenation, nurturing, rest, and love for your family. On top of this, you will also be expected to be sexually appealing, a good cook, a great mother, and physically, emotionally, and spiritually fit. It's overwhelming to most women, but the good news is that you don't have to do it all on your own. You can seek God's help.[24]

Deceptive Statements

Let's end this triage with three excerpts from a book that has led many women down a deceptive path. Do these statements agree with what Scripture teaches? What is God's ultimate goal for you? How does that affect your pursuit of good theology? Do our fathers and husbands mediate God's Word to us? And how does this author's teaching on headship differ from God's Word?

Excerpt: God's ultimate goal for you is to meet your man's needs. God's original intention was that a woman would spend her life helping her husband fulfill his dreams and ambitions.[25]

Excerpt: When our first daughter was just two months away from getting married, she asked her daddy a theological question. . . . He told her, "I cannot answer your Bible questions, for you now believe what your husband believes. He will be your head, and you will follow him. It is time to get adjusted to your new role. Ask him what he believes about it."[26]

24. Omartian, *Power of a Praying Wife*, 37.
25. Debi Pearl, *Created to Be His Help Meet: Discover How God Can Make Your Marriage Glorious* (Pleasantville, TN: No Greater Joy Ministries, 2004), 162.
26. Ibid., 231.

Excerpt: But first, know that a husband has authority to tell his wife what to wear, where to go, whom to talk to, how to spend her time, when to speak and when not to, even if he is unreasonable and insensitive, but he does not have authority to command her to view pornography with him or to assist him in the commission of a crime.[27]

27. Ibid., 260.

PREACHING TO WOMEN AND
SITTING UNDER THE WORD[1]

In my early twenties I was asked to teach a women's Bible study, and I was in way over my head. As the co-owner of a coffee shop, I had begun to meet many women from the different churches in my town. I've never been much of a small-talker, so the discussions that we began having about the implications of our faith in the different stages of life we were in led a few women to ask me to lead a more purposeful study. And yet

---

1. I will always remember where I was for my fortieth birthday. It fell on a Tuesday, so the most I was hoping for was an awesome dinner at my favorite Thai restaurant in Shepherdstown, West Virginia. (I live in Frederick, Maryland, which has a beautiful downtown filled with excellent restaurants. But, yes, West Virginia still holds my award for best Thai nearby. Definitely check out Kazus if you ever get the chance.) I was going to wait for a weekend celebration with my friends to help me mark such an anxious milestone. But then, a couple of months before that looming day, David Silvernail asked me to speak to his Communications and Preaching class at Reformed Theological Seminary in Washington, DC, on the topic of preaching to women. It just happened to fall on that particular Tuesday. I figured that a housewife theologian in seminary talking with pastors-in-training would inaugurate my fortieth year pretty well. So this chapter is a result of that experience. It is the talk I gave, adapted for a book, with an added section for women about sitting under the preached Word.

the reason I was so good at striking up these conversations was because I had a lot to learn. I wasn't really equipped to teach, especially not to teach women coming from all the different churches in our town. Our small group represented Methodist, Pentecostal, Baptist, Presbyterian, and Roman Catholic women, as well as some young women who had never been much into church. Thankfully, my pastor invited me to teach it as a small group of our church. My husband and I were at a Baptist church at that time. This was such a relief to me, as I was looking forward to being under the guidance of the elders for such a task.

I quickly noticed that, with all the presuppositions we were bringing to the text, it would be helpful to teach a series on the doctrine of Scripture before we got into studying particular books of the Bible. And as I began asking questions, my pastor suggested a systematic theology book that he thought would be helpful to teach from. It was organized well for beginners and provided questions for further study after each chapter. However, when I got to the teaching on the sufficiency of Scripture, things weren't lining up for me. This author was teaching that Scripture is the sufficient Word of God to us, but was also teaching that we could receive authoritative prophecies containing new, personal revelation. So I once again went to my pastor with some questions.

As I began pointing out the inconsistencies to my pastor, genuinely wanting to learn which was true—is Scripture sufficient, or are we to look for further revelation?—he reacted in a surprising way. He laughed it off, saying something like, "Aimee, I think you're going a little too deep with this women's study." He basically told me that he didn't expect us to learn *that* much, and that I shouldn't worry my pretty little head over such deep theological matters.

Why is this story relevant to the topic of preaching? Because I represent the person whom you are trying to reach on Sunday morning and whom you will be pastoring throughout the week. I'm the reason why you go to seminary. Your seminary professors haven't advanced your education so that you can merely talk to other academics about preaching. Your congregation should benefit from your seminary investment, right? As a woman, I represent more than half the church. And preaching to women involves more than a few tips for when you're behind the pulpit. There are important steps in preparation.

Reductionist Stereotyping

So I want to begin by asking you a question. What are your expectations for your congregation? In the sermon-letter to the Hebrews, we see the writer saying,

> About this we have much to say, and it is hard to explain, since you have become dull of hearing. For though by this time you ought to be teachers, you need someone to teach you again the basic principles of the oracles of God. You need milk, not solid food, for everyone who lives on milk is unskilled in the word of righteousness, since he is a child. But solid food is for the mature, for those who have their powers of discernment trained by constant practice to distinguish good from evil.
>
> Therefore let us leave the elementary doctrine of Christ and go on to maturity, not laying again a foundation of repentance from dead works and of faith toward God, and of instruction about washings, the laying on of hands, the resurrection of the dead, and eternal judgment. (5:11–6:2)

Here the preacher to the Hebrews is making an assessment of his first audience to this sermon-letter. We see that the preacher is disappointed that they are not as theologically mature as he thinks they should be. And he wants to move past the foundation that he has already laid in order to further equip them. What is this rich theology that he wants to teach? Recent scholarship suggests that Hebrews is a sermon-letter based on Psalm 110.[2] This admonishment to maturity and warning against apostasy is within the context of the preacher's exposition of what I'd call the pinnacle of Psalm 110—verse 4: "The Lord has sworn and will not change his mind, 'You are a priest forever after the order of Melchizedek.'" That's some pretty serious theology! The preacher's expectations are high.

And yet what does he tell them? He tells them they are dull of hearing and immature in the faith. They should be teachers themselves at this point, but they need admonishment to theological fitness if they are going to persevere. They need their powers of discernment trained by constant practice in order to distinguish good from evil. So we see an honest evaluation here. But the preacher to the Hebrews does not reduce his message. No, he feeds them with a theologically rich sermon to build the confession of their hope, and he exhorts them to hold fast to that. He equips them to know Jesus as Lord in both his person and his work.

Getting back to my experience, my pastor's laugh reduced me as a person made in the image of God. It reduced me to a stereotype, and it sent the message that my pastor expected me to go only so far in my learning. And I was the teacher of the only women's Bible study in the church at the time. So what message does that send about the level of theological and spiritual growth that he projected for all the women in his church?

What are your expectations for your congregation? What are your expectations *for the women* in your congregation?

---

2. George Wesley Buchanan, *To the Hebrews*, The Anchor Bible 36 (Garden City, NY: Doubleday, 1972), xix, quoted in Dennis E. Johnson, *Him We Proclaim: Preaching Christ from All the Scriptures* (Phillipsburg, NJ: P&R, 2007), 178.

This will show in your preaching, whether you have thought about it or not. If you want your preaching to connect with the women in the congregation, you first need to have high expectations for them to mature in the Word.

Listen to Them

And if you do have these expectations, then their questions will be important to you and their input will be valuable to you. So another important part of sermon preparation is listening. You of course need to get to know your congregation in order to pastor them well. Don't depend on your wife to know the women in your church. Sure, your wife can provide valuable insight that you may not pick up, but your wife is not their pastor—you are. One of your best tools to connect the message of your sermon to the women sitting in the pews is to know the blessings and the challenges that they are facing in their everyday lives of faith and obedience.

Connected to this is the importance of *asking them questions*. If I stop at the church during the week for some reason, I know that poking my head into my pastor's office to say "hi" will likely lead to him asking me questions. There are the basic, obligatory pastoral questions about how my family and I are doing. But, more often than not, he will ask me questions based on the text he is preparing to preach from. He wants to know what comes to our minds as we encounter the text, and he does this by asking pointed questions. This makes him a better preacher.

One thing that I appreciate about the way my pastor asks questions is that he doesn't presume to have all the answers. He's not quizzing us. He wrestles with the text, not just to come up with a doctrinal formulation to enlighten us with, but because he is working to fit it in with the whole of Scripture, to lead us to Christ, and to equip us with God's Word to go out into the world as faithful servants. By doing this, he is even teaching me to be a better teacher of others.

So, for example, one day when I was at the church picking weeds, he was preparing to preach on Matthew 6:16–17, which deals with fasting. So Francis started talking about the difficulty of preaching on fasting these days. It just so happened that I had had a conversation with a young woman only days beforehand regarding her secret struggle with anorexia. Francis asked a few questions, which opened the door for me to mention that he might want to consider that some women in our congregation might have eating disorders. This meant that they might attach a different meaning to the word *fasting* when they heard it. Maybe I was only confirming something he had already thought about addressing in the sermon, but, when I sat under his preaching and heard the way that he incorporated this concern as an application of the text, he communicated more than the fact that he is a good listener. He communicated that he cares about the women in the church and their brokenness. He communicated that he is their pastor and that Christ's words are for them, too.

But Francis doesn't ask only me questions; he is that way with everyone. As a result, those who may have seen him during the week, or who may have received an email or phone call from him, come to hear the Word having already begun contemplating the Scripture that he is about to preach on. By asking questions while preparing his sermon, Francis is already preparing our minds and hearts for the sermon.

Our Brains

Do women process information differently from men, and should you take this into consideration when it comes to preparing your sermons? There is all kinds of research that points to the differences between the male and female brains. But, as soon as you begin looking into that, you will find all kinds of research debunking that research. Yes, there are some proven neurological differences between the brains of men and women, but how that transfers into the way that we process information, interact, and learn can be tricky. One popular teaching is that men systematize and women empathize. While there seems to be some generally observable truth in this, there are also many exceptions.

One of the biggest complaints that I hear from women who have left complementarianism and joined egalitarian churches is that they felt like they didn't fit inside the box that the teaching on "biblical womanhood" put them in. We don't need to add extrabiblical labels to women and then try to have them live up to those imposed standards. I share this finding in order to encourage you to preach well-rounded sermons, without making statements about all women or all men.

The systematizers will love your sermon outline. They will look at your three points, or whatever you've got there, and will know what to be listening for and how to categorize what you are saying. They may even enjoy a conversation with you about the chiastic structure of the text after the sermon.

Your empathizers may or may not look at that carefully planned sermon outline. They are studying the look in your eye as you deliver your opening hook. They pay attention to the shifting of the tone of your voice and the dramatic pauses. And then they are going to want to engage with the perspectives of the people involved in the text. While the systematizers may pay attention to your shift in movement while you transition to the next important point, the empathizers are engaging all of their senses and are more abstract in the way that they process the sermon.

But here's the thing: we don't all fit so neatly into these categories. I would love to hear about the chiastic structure of the text. Does that make me masculine? Of course not. But when I look at the best sellers list for women in the Christian market, I see that we are targeted for our empathetic tendencies. In surveying the books for men, I see more of a systematic approach. And if these books are selling so well, then there must be something to this.

But the market is doing us a disservice by over-pandering to these distinctions. It's amazing how often it helps to return to the first several chapters in Genesis when I am studying something. Let's look at Genesis 1:27 as we are talking about preaching to women: "So God created man in his own image, in the image of God he created him; male and female he created them." We all reflect the image of God, both the so-called systematizers and the so-called empathizers. And we need to learn from each other. Does a man who is nurturing and emotionally intelligent lack masculinity? No! I believe that he is maturing as a man in the image of God. Is a woman who can parallel park like a boss and write a killer business plan unfeminine? Does that make her less of a woman?

Clearly God has designed us differently. And yet, as Dorothy Sayers has written, "The fundamental thing is that women are more like men than anything else in the world."[3] Together we make up the image of God. We need both! Sure, there are some distinctions that preachers should be considering when they are teaching. But we need to be well rounded as we grow in maturity. Your sermons should reflect that.

The thing is, I've got bad news. Who can understand women? I'm not going to be able to solve the mystery for you. Songwriters and poets have been trying to figure out women

---

3. Dorothy Sayers, *Are Women Human?* (Grand Rapids: Eerdmans, 1971), 53.

since time began. Adam's first response to the creation of Eve was a beautiful poem: "This at last is bone of my bones and flesh of my flesh; she shall be called Woman, because she was taken out of Man" (Gen. 2:23).

Perhaps Billy Joel captures the best description of women after the fall in his song "She's Always a Woman." We're complicated. But he makes an astute observation when he makes the point that women bring out the best and the worst in men. That's what I want you to think about as you prepare to preach to women. It's so true! Communicate well to us. Invest in that. The more you learn about us, sure, you may not be any closer to figuring us out, but it will make you a better pastor. We can bring out the best in you, and we can bring out the worst in you!

I can identify with Billy Joel's song. People say a lot about women and what makes us feminine—especially in the church. But even if a woman doesn't exhibit all the so-called feminine traits that are expected of her, she's always a woman. And you can't nail her down. Don't even try; that's when you will reduce her.

The Diversity of Women

We are a diverse group. Let me help you by laying out some common roles that many of us share, which men do not. I am not teaching you anything new here but am reminding you of the many roles that are unique to women. But notice: even within these roles that we have in common, there is great diversity.

Daughters

Men will never experience being a daughter. And yet there are many differences within this one role that men can relate to. Among the daughters in your church you will have only children, daughters from big households, daughters from households with varying income, differences in the number of parents and stepparents that daughters have, foster daughters, stepdaughters, and adopted daughters. And this role can significantly change from one culture to another. To be a daughter in the United States has a different value from being a daughter in China, for example. This is something to consider in your pastoring.

Sisters

Sisterhood is a wonderful bond that men do not share. However, you have the privilege of brotherhood. These roles also vary according to whether the women are from urban, suburban, rural, or international settings.

Aunts

Many women have the privilege of being aunts. This is admittedly different from the privilege of being an uncle. Foremost, we all know how to pronounce the word *uncle*. But with women, we like to complicate things. Is it pronounced *ant* or *ahnt*? We will probably never clear that up!

Wives

Men may be husbands, but they will never be wives. You will preach to many wives, but please do not put them all in the same idealistic category. Sure, you will have your idealistic marriages with flourishing women, but many of the wives sitting under your preaching will actually be quite lonely. Maybe they will be married to an unbeliever or a workaholic. You will have wives of alcoholics and porn addicts, wives of mama's boys, and wives of controlling men. You will have married women in abusive marriages. How will all this affect your preaching?

Mothers

The same goes for mothers. You will have women who desperately hope to be mothers but cannot conceive; you will have broken, single mothers who can hardly keep their heads above water, mothers devastated by a rebellious child, mothers who have suffered miscarriage, competitive mothers, working moms, stay-at-home moms, many overwhelmed moms, casserole moms, organic, cage-free, non-GMO, gluten-free, essential oil moms, empty nesters, and grandmothers. God calls a diverse group of mothers to his church, and you pastor them all.

Grandmothers

What an honor it must be for grandparents to participate in the next generation of their family! Some grandmothers are able to spend a lot of time with their grandchildren, while others may be hindered by the physical distance, emotional distance, or even spiritual distance from their children. A wise and experienced grandmother is such a gift to the church. How can you encourage her to share her wisdom? Many will be exhausted as they find themselves helping with their grandchildren while also caring for their elderly parents. What comfort can they find in the gospel at this stage of life? And what about the widows who have basic practical needs they could use help with, while also longing for some more company?

Sisters in Christ

This one is especially practical for you. Paul tells Timothy how to relate to his congregation as a pastor:

> Do not rebuke an older man but encourage him as you would a father, younger men as brothers, older women as mothers, younger women as sisters, in all purity. (1 Tim. 5:1–2)

You may not be a mother, but you have a mother. You know how a mother is to be treated. This is how you are to relate to the older women in your church. You will never be a sister, but you may have biological sisters. If not, you are still very familiar with the relationship between brothers and sisters. And you have many mothers and sisters in the church. How would you preach to your mother? How would you preach to your sister? How would you pastor them?

Thinking this way will help you to be in touch with the issues that are going to concern them. When someone in our family is going through a trial or being tempted by a particular sin, we are passionate to engage with them and to help them in this area. So, if you notice that your little sister is placing her meaning and her value in the praise and attention she is getting from a guy, you are going to want to teach her more about her identity in Christ and help her to spot those idols in her life. If your sister is in an abusive relationship and is too ashamed and scared to ask for help, a loving brother will notice that something isn't right. She is going to need to learn about Christ's love for his bride, the church, and how a marriage points to this. What if your sister is trying to be a good friend to someone else who is in an abusive relationship? This will be an issue that is dear to her heart.

As you see your mother going through the different stages of parenting, your heart will go out to her when she packs her last school lunch and carpools for the last time. What does she do with all those memories and life lessons? What is her vocation now? A son knows the value of an experienced, wise, godly woman. He wants to share that with others and minister to her in her time of need.

Many of your sisters in Christ will experience issues such as loneliness, loss of a sense of worth, negative body image, betrayal, sexual assault, dating and friendship, hormonal imbalances, infertility, miscarriage, fatigue, depression, adulterous spouses, rebellious children, temptation to live for the world, questions about their contribution to society, difficulty with aging, and responsibilities in taking care of others. These are all issues that can be addressed from the pulpit in application as you faithfully preach through Scripture. This is ordinary life for women. Be their brother in Christ from the pulpit—and outside the pulpit.

Of course, you are even more than a brother. You will hold a special office as pastor—a gift to us from the Lord for "building up the body of Christ, until we all attain to the unity of the faith and of the knowledge of the Son of God" (Eph. 4:12–13). There is plenty of topical teaching aimed at women who are going through many of the experiences I just mentioned. And that can be a great help to us. But we are called out on the first day of every week to corporate worship, and we come needing the Word of God to be preached to us. Please faithfully preach through the Word. I'm not against a topical sermon or series when a pastor sees a need in his church, but the regular expectation should be expository preaching of the Word. No matter what trial men or women are going through, we all need the Word. This is what Paul tells Timothy:

> I charge you in the presence of God and of Christ Jesus, who is to judge the living and the dead, and by his appearing and his kingdom: preach the word; be ready in season and out of season; reprove, rebuke, and exhort, with complete patience and teaching. For the time is coming when people will not endure sound teaching, but having itching ears they will accumulate for themselves teachers to suit their own passions, and will turn away from listening to the truth and wander off into myths. As for you, always be sober-minded, endure suffering, do the work of an evangelist, fulfill your ministry. (2 Tim. 4:1–5)

Right before that charge in 2 Timothy are the verses that I've been discussing in this book, in which Paul addresses some of the troubling issues concerning the women in the church. False teachers are targeting them, as they go on to influence the rest of the congregation. There are "little women" who are caught up in sin, idle with the free time they are afforded, and easy prey for dividing a church. After that, he reminds Timothy of two women who had a profound influence on him—who, like Paul, taught him the sacred writings, which are able to make him wise for salvation. These are his mother and grandmother, who have acquainted him with the true Word since his childhood.

Notice that Paul doesn't then encourage Timothy to begin a series of sermons on false teaching or how to catechize our kids. No, he tells him to preach the Word, both when it's popular and when it's not. When we think we need to hear about a certain topic, what we really need is the living Word, which cuts like a scalpel. Paul declares, "All Scripture is breathed out by God and profitable for teaching, for reproof, for correction, and for training in righteousness" (2 Tim. 3:16).

Depend on the Spirit, who will not let God's Word go out void to all your sisters and brothers in Christ.

Practical Tips

Moving on to a more practical note, a brother *makes eye contact*. This goes a long way when preaching to women. The key to empathy is looking someone in the eye, right? You can find out a lot about people by what their eyes say. You are preaching a message with your eyes, whether you know it or not. Ralph Waldo Emerson said, "An eye can threaten like a loaded and levelled gun, or can insult like hissing or kicking; or in its altered mood by beams of kindness it can make the heart dance with joy." And, "The eyes of men converse as much as their tongues, with the advantage that the ocular dialect needs no dictionary, but is understood all the world over. When the eyes say one thing and the tongue another, a practised man relies on the language of the first."[4]

Communication with your eyes is just as important as, if not more important than, what is coming out of your mouth. You could spend all week putting together a well-polished sermon, but if your eyes don't communicate the passion of your message, you can lose us in the first thirty seconds.

Good eye contact also helps you to gauge how well you are connecting. You will be able to tell whether we are leaning in with interest or waiting for you to wrap up. This will help you to reevaluate later. Have you noticed whether you are getting equal eye contact from both the men and the women? Do you find that you tend to be more comfortable making eye contact with men when you preach? If so, why is that? You may have a comfort-level issue when it comes to making appropriate eye contact with women. Reminding yourself that they are your sisters and your mothers will likely go a long way in helping you to communicate well in this way.

Maybe you will notice that it's easier to make eye contact with the older women, or maybe you will find it easier to connect in this way with the disadvantaged women out of empathy. Whatever is the case, pay attention. If I am a woman sitting in your congregation and I notice that you never make eye contact with me, I am going to wonder what it is about me that keeps you from looking me in the eye. You want to be careful that you are not sending an inadvertent message

---

4. Ralph Waldo Emerson, "The Conduct of Life," in *The Works of Ralph Waldo Emerson*, vol. 1 (Boston: Jefferson Press, 1888), 171 and 173. The entire book can be accessed online at https://books.google.com/books?id=E-NDAAAAYAAJ& source=gbs_navlinks_s.

to women that they are a threat, like some disease to be avoided—or, even worse, that they are completely ignorable. Make sure that your eyes and your tongue are in sync. Women are perceptive and intuitive. Make sure you are working the whole room, as they say. And, of course, don't overthink this and be creepy! Back when I used to own a coffee shop, I had a regular customer named Dennis. Dennis was a professional, friendly guy, who basically ordered the same thing every day. But that wasn't the only thing predictable about Dennis. Even though he was well liked by all of us baristas, we had a running joke that Dennis must have taken the Dale Carnegie training courses. He would come in the door, and we would greet him with a "Hi, Dennis, how are you today?" And without fail he would look his greeter in the eye like it was his job and reply, "I'm fine; how are you?" And then there was the awkward pause as his robotic eye contact and forced smile stayed locked, we swore, as he silently counted to himself, "One, two, three." Then he would become normal again and make his usual order. Don't be a Dennis.

Another practical tip: *use feminine pronouns*. We can easily give away our stereotypes in our illustrations. I'm not sitting back and looking for a pastor to use feminine pronouns when he is describing someone intelligent or ambitious, but my ears perk up when he does because I am so conditioned to hearing masculine pronouns for those illustrations. That immediately sends a message to me.

Also, there will be women in your congregation who have been or are in abusive relationships. You need to think about this in your sermon delivery. While it is good to use a solemn or authoritative voice in your teaching sometimes, remember that gentleness and kindness also need to be communicated from the pulpit. You want your demeanor from the pulpit to signify that you are someone who is safe to learn from and to go to for help. Think about this in your illustrations as well. You may have no idea how encouraging it could be to use something as simple as a feminine pronoun when describing someone with dignity or someone with the wisdom to seek good counsel.

If your expectations are high, you are going to *stimulate women to think* from the pulpit. Point out their need and responsibility to be competent theologians in all their roles—as daughters, sisters, friends, students, employees, employers, neighbors, wives, mothers, caretakers, and so on. What they believe to be true about God and themselves will shape their everyday decision making and behavior. But, more than that, it is an eternal matter. Impress the truth upon both the women and the men that they are theologians. We all have some sort of knowledge about God. The question is whether we are good theologians or poor ones. We are called to a life of faith and obedience. How does our knowledge of who the Lord is and what he has done on our behalf affect us?

Women have a powerful influence both in our personal households and in the household of God. Maybe there are women in your church who do not see the significance of their vocation. In his autobiography, the great nineteenth-century preacher, Charles Spurgeon, extols a fascinating woman whom we may think didn't have a very influential position:

> The first lessons I ever had in theology were from an old cook in the school at Newmarket where I was an usher. She was a good old soul, and used to read *The Gospel Standard*. . . . She lived strongly as well as fed strongly . . . and I do believe that I learnt more from her than I should have learned from any six doctors of divinity of the sort we have nowadays. There are some Christian people who taste, and see, and enjoy religion in their own souls, and who get at a deeper

knowledge of it than books can ever give them, though they should search all their days. The cook at Newmarket was a godly experienced woman, from whom I learned far more than I did from the minister of the chapel we attended.[5]

John Wesley, the pastor who is well known for starting the Methodist movement with his brother and hymn writer, Charles, is commonly quoted as saying, "I learned more about Christianity from my mother than from all the theologians in England." Our theology matters. Women are influential in their relationships. Press this truth upon them in your sermons. Encourage them and equip them to point others to Christ.

Now let's get back to my opening illustration. Preaching to women shouldn't be disconnected from pastoring women. One thing that I was thankful to that pastor for was that he didn't just give me the latest best-selling book for women in the church. He originally suggested that I read a systematic theology book. He also lent me some of his commentaries. That led me to love theology books. It also helped equip me to recognize and discern the bad theology that is marketed to women.

I am thankful that there are some solid books written by women for women. They will be a blessing to your church. But encourage the women in your congregation to read widely. Also, I encourage you yourself to read widely in a way that you may not have considered: *read books written for women.* This will make you a better pastor. Know the environment of the Christian market, and learn from what the women in your church are reading. If it is troublesome, you need to know! And it would be great if you had books that you could recommend.

5. C. H. Spurgeon, *Autobiography*, vol. 1, *The Early Years: 1834–1859* (Carlisle, PA: Banner of Truth Trust, 1962), 38–39.

Commit to reading one or two books a year that are written for women in the church. One of the most rewarding things for me as an author is when a pastor tells me that he has read something that I have written and explains how that has helped him to relate better to the women in his own congregation. By doing this, you will show the women in the church that you really do care about them, that they are not peripheral or sidelined, and that what they care about and what they are learning matters.

Eschatological Perspective

So what is your expectation for the women in your church? What is Christ's expectation for us? Together, believing men and women make up the body of Christ. Regardless of all our differences, we are all united to Jesus by his Holy Spirit, sharing the common goal of serving him for eternity. Scripture tells us that Christ is interceding on our behalf this very moment, sovereignly working to transform us into his likeness. We are the bride of Christ, awaiting his return and the consummation of his kingdom. So you're not just relating to your sisters in Christ in the tension of living between the already and the not yet; you are relating to eternal beings who, like you, will be given resurrected bodies to serve together in the new heavens and the new earth.

How is your preaching helping to prepare us for that day? What will our relationships and learning be like then? As we think about our final goal—men and women joyfully serving our Lord Jesus together—it affects the way that we relate now, doesn't it?

So preach to women with an eschatological perspective, knowing that, even with all our differences, we have the most important thing of all in common. We are so used to hearing that men are from Mars and women are from Venus, but this saying sets us up for failure because, no matter what our differences may be, we are all humans made in the image of God and in need of a Savior. We all need to hear that in sin we have offended our Creator, our holy God, and that his law is good and we have broken it. But with great love, before the beginning of time, our God made an intra-Trinitarian covenant to redeem a people for himself. The Father promised the Son a bride. The Son promised to fulfill the terms of the covenant on our behalf. And he has! He has come, perfectly fulfilling all righteousness and sacrificing himself on our behalf, giving the perfect thank offering of himself to the Father, while also paying the full penalty for the sin of all those who believe. And the Holy Spirit promises to apply those benefits to the beloved of God! The preached Word is a means of grace for all of us who have been given eyes to see and ears to hear.

Preach with great expectation, knowing that God's Word doesn't go forth void! Preach with the knowledge that he is bringing in all his people, calling us to repentance and to lives of faith and obedience as new creations. Preach with the expectation that you will be worshipping and serving beside the very people in your congregation, in resurrected bodies, for eternity! Preach with the knowledge that women are necessary allies and that we need to be prepared for that great day with the same care that men are.

Sitting under the Word

It's appropriate to end this book by talking about one of the most important things that we do in life: sitting under the preached Word. There is a disconnect between the good preaching that many women sit under and the teaching that some of those very same women are eager to absorb throughout the week. While this is a problem that pastors need to investigate and consider in their shepherding, it is also something that should cause self-examination for us women.

I do hope that this doesn't come off as condescending. You may find it patronizing for me to end a book for competent women on the topic of how to listen well, especially after I've spent many pages on how to read well. These are basic skills that we learned a long time ago. My daughter learned how to sit up on her own at four months old. But I am finding myself reminding her now, in her teenage years, about the way she is supposed to sit. It's all too easy to fall into a habit of slouching, and over time that can wreak havoc on your body. Are we slouching under the Word?

We may be pretty darn proud of ourselves for getting our family through the door every Sunday. Sure, my son's clothes could have used ironing and he's got some dried toothpaste on his mouth, my husband and I have argued with the girls about interesting wardrobe choices and then argued with each other about where the checkbook is, and no one has bothered to feed the dog until we ask on our way out the door. But we get there. Every week we manage to win the game show challenge of making it to church. Now we can fellowship, join in the singing and liturgy, and sit back and absorb godliness by osmosis after those wonderful words, "You may now be seated." We've held up our end of the deal, and now it's time for the pastor to do what we pay him to do. But listening isn't a passive activity, especially when we are talking about the Word of God. In his book *Expository Listening*, Ken Ramey warns us, "Every time you hear the Word of God preached, you are training yourself to either obey or disobey God."[6]

---

6. Ken Ramey, *Expository Listening: A Handbook for Hearing and Doing God's Word* (The Woodlands, TX: Kress Biblical Resources, 2010), 98.

We know what it means to be a good listener when we are the ones speaking, just as I know how a person is supposed to sit when I see my daughter slouching. But we often forget that we need to keep training ourselves. So I am going to remind us here what we are actually doing when we sit under the Word and how we can stay active and get the most out of it. Let's end this book with some simple principles to help us to be competent listeners who are so trained by the Word that those thirty minutes or so of sitting may be the most active part of our week. There are three things for us to keep in mind as active listeners of the Word: we are called to hear God's Word, we are to engage with his Word, and his Word sends us back out into the world.

Called to Hear God's Word

We aren't just going to church on Sundays. And we aren't just assembling together with fellow believers to offer our worship to God. On the first day of every week, we are interrupting our everyday living and being called out as a people to a covenant renewal ceremony. God's people live under the covenant of grace. We aren't only looking back to the amazing work of Christ in his incarnation, righteous life, atonement, resurrection, and ascension. We are looking forward to something—the new heavens and the new earth. We are new creations, regenerated by his Spirit, living between the already of the inauguration of Christ's kingdom and the not yet of its consummation. We are part of something incredible when God calls us to our Sunday worship service—the future breaking into the present! We get so caught up in our busyness and our own goals and issues throughout the week that we continuously return to our default of thinking that it's all about us. But there is something much more grand and wondrous happening that we are privileged to participate in.

And we need to be reminded. The gospel message is

something that is outside of us; it is something that we need to hear continually. On Sunday, we are called to hear from God. Our pastor preaches with the authority of the Word of God. How does that change the way in which we come to hear it? How does that affect our demeanor? First of all, we should want to prepare ourselves to hear a word from God. Do we pray for our pastor throughout the week while he is preparing his sermon? Do we regard it as a privilege to gather as God's covenant community? If we do, we will want to be alert when we arrive. For some of us, that means that we need more sleep the night before. How many hours does it take you to wake up in the morning? Plan to wake up in plenty of time for you to be attentive when you arrive. Another way to be prepared is to read ahead of time the passage of Scripture that your pastor will be preaching on and to meditate on it beforehand. Think of it as a warm-up for the workout that is ahead. Your mind and heart will come ready to engage. And, if we know that we are coming for God's Word, we should also come expecting that we will be blessed in Christ by the preaching of the Word. God's Word is "operative"; it "is ever doing something."[7] We will be changed by it one way or another.

Engaging with God's Word

No, we aren't just called out to sit like targets for God's words to shoot at and land wherever they may. We get to actively engage with God's Word. Interestingly, good posture when we sit can help us with breathing and alertness. Sitting up attentively also sends a message to the preacher. Engaging with the preacher through eye contact, posture, and nonverbal gestures enables him to see where he is connecting and encourages him that you are in fact listening and are not making up your grocery list in

---

7. Edward Reynolds, *An Explication of the Hundred and Tenth Psalm* (London, 1837; repr., London: Forgotten Books, 2015), 5.

your head. Ask yourself related questions while you are hearing the Word and jot them down for later. Taking notes may serve to help you retain teaching and refer back to it later. Rather than taking notes on a bulletin that will eventually get tossed, perhaps a journal that contains your reflections, the questions that the sermon provoked, and related Scriptures for further study could be a real gem that you'll want to keep. But maybe writing notes during the sermon distracts you from the sacramental element of hearing God's Word to his people, making it feel more like a lecture. There is debate about that. Even if you don't take notes during the sermon, it certainly would be beneficial to journal afterwards. One way or another, we need to engage with the Word like the Bereans, who were called "more noble" because "they received the word with all eagerness, examining the Scriptures daily to see if these things were so" (Acts 17:11). Do we receive the Word with eagerness? I sure hope so. Besides, we have a responsibility as a covenant community to affirm that the pastor's words are in line with God's Word.

Sending Us Back Out into the World

But it isn't over when the pastor prays and we sing that last song. At the end of each service, our pastor sends us back into the world with a benediction. We receive this blessing from the Lord in order for us to bear the fruit of the preached Word according to the work of Christ, so that we can in turn be a blessing in his name. God's Word is still active when we are getting back in our cars and driving home. Our pastor should be able to say the same thing about us that Paul wrote to the Corinthian church:

> You yourselves are our letter of recommendation, written on our hearts, to be known and read by all. And you show that you are a letter from Christ delivered by us, written not

with ink but with the Spirit of the living God, not on tablets of stone but on tablets of human hearts. (2 Cor. 3:2–3)

God's people hear his voice, hide his Word in their hearts, and establish themselves in it.

Do you see the fruit of the preached Word in your life? Delighting in and meditating on the preached Word is the blessing. The person who does that is described as a mature, glorious tree "planted by streams of water that yields its fruit in its season, and its leaf does not wither. In all that he does, he prospers" (Ps. 1:3). God has planted us in Christ. We can drink from his Word and meditate on it. That means that we won't only read and hear it but will listen to it, study it, learn from it, share it, and teach it. And what will happen? We will bring forth spiritual fruit in its proper season. Spurgeon declares that the godly man brings forth "not unseasonable graces, like untimely figs, which are never full-flavoured. But the man who delights in God's Word, being taught by it, bringeth forth patience in the time of suffering, faith in the day of trial, and holy joy in the hour of prosperity."[8] Because God has planted us in Christ, this will happen. All these fruits are blessedness. But the supreme blessing will be that beatific vision of Jesus Christ in his full glory. Our future hope gives us joy in the present.

It is our joy to sit under the preached Word as we wait for that glorious day. Let us be like those in Antioch when they heard Christ preached. As Paul and Barnabas "went out, the people begged that these things might be told them the next Sabbath" (Acts 13:42). That is receiving the Word with eagerness. After all, we are people of the Word, and we look forward to him tabernacling with us for eternity.

8. Charles H. Spurgeon, *The Treasury of David*, vol. 1, *Psalms 1–57* (repr., Peabody, MA: Hendrickson Publishers, 1990), 2.

Questions for Reflection and Discussion

1. What are your expectations, as a church member, for your spiritual and theological maturity? Where do you expect to be one year, five years, and twenty years from now? What are your expectations when you come to worship every Sunday? *Pastors,* what are your expectations for growing as an officer in the church? What are your expectations for your congregation? For the women in your congregation?

2. Do you tend to systematize or empathize? Describe the weakness in leaning too far one way or the other. How can you balance your own tendencies? *Pastors,* do you think that your sermons are geared more to one way of thinking or to the other?

3. List all the different roles that you fulfill as a woman. How do you think they affect the way in which you engage with a sermon? What major similarities do we all share and need to have tended to by the preached Word?

4. Did any of the practical tips in this chapter stand out to you? Do you have any more that would be helpful to add?

5. How does your view of the new heavens and the new earth affect your relationships within the church and your learning now? *Pastors,* how is your preaching and pastoring geared toward helping us to prepare for that day?

6. You are called out along with the rest of God's covenant community to assemble and hear his Word preached. How does this affect the way that you come prepared to hear it and engage with it? Does it really make a difference for you the following Wednesday? If the research is right, we remember only about ten percent or less of a sermon after we leave. Will that really make any lasting difference five years from now?